How to run children's clubs and meetings

Practical suggestions for people in youth ministry

© Day One Publications 2007
First printed 2007

ISBN 978-1-84625-060-6

9 781846 250606 >

ISBN 978-1-84625-060-6

British Library Cataloguing in Publication Data available

Published by Day One Publications
Ryelands Road, Leominster, HR6 8NZ
☎ 01568 613 740 FAX 01568 611 473
email—sales@dayone.co.uk
web site—www.dayone.co.uk
North American—e-mail—sales@dayonebookstore.com
North American—web site—www.dayonebookstore.com

Designed by Steve Devane and printed by Gutenberg Press, Malta

To all my fellow half-term clubbers,
to all my former fellow Friday- and Teens-Clubbers,
and in particular to Brian Ventress,
whose friendship over the last twenty-six years
has been of enormous value and influence.

Thanks

Several friends, Adrian Davies, Heather Ricketts, and Brian Ventress, have been kind enough to read some draft chapters of this book and to make helpful comments upon it, and I would like to thank them for their time and observations. I owe the greatest debt, however, to Paul Brown. He has been extremely generous with his time in reading and editing my manuscript, and the feedback he gave was constructive, frank, and gracious.

I am also very grateful to Suzanne Mitchell, who has edited my manuscript and made a number of helpful amendments to clarify my meaning and to improve the way in which I have phrased things. The idea of including a summary at the end of each chapter was also hers, and I am sure that this will greatly help to crystallize the points raised.

Contents

Why this book?

W e would love to see people appear out of the blue who are superbly gifted at working with children and teenagers. They would explain things very simply, and show the children what the passage means for *them*. The children would listen eagerly as they spoke. These workers would have unlimited energy and patience, and be highly organized so that everything ran with barely a hitch.

Unfortunately, people like this are extremely rare. If we do nothing ourselves other than wait for them to appear, we will probably be disappointed. My own pastor sometimes says that if a job is worth doing, it is worth doing *badly*. He means that it is better to *attempt* something with limited skill and resources than simply not to bother. God's kingdom often grows through people of limited ability who do their best. Perhaps at the moment your own church does not hold a meeting or club for children. Or maybe it does run such an activity, but needs more helpers. You could assist, but wonder whether you have what it takes. This book will hopefully help you to make a start. Perhaps you already help with a children's club or meeting, but often feel that you are simply muddling along. This book is designed to help make you more effective.

If a job is worth doing, it is also worth doing *well*. Any service for the Lord deserves our very best efforts. We should continually try to improve, whether we are new to sharing the gospel with children or have been doing so for a number of years. Hopefully this book will contain some tips and ideas for fairly experienced workers.

My aim is to be *practical*, and at the end of some chapters I have suggested ways in which you could develop and practise the specific skills highlighted within the chapters. I would especially encourage you to try those activities that relate to an area where you feel weak. Using these as a starting point, you may find it helpful to devise your own 'exercises', to gain further practice.

A word of clarification

The teaching of God's Word to children takes place within a range of settings, both within the context of a local church and by other groups of Christians—Sunday schools, holiday Bible clubs, and midweek meetings—and the forms that these activities take vary considerably. This book should help those involved in any type of children's work, although some parts will be more relevant to one kind of meeting than to others.

The term 'children' is used throughout in the sense of 'under eighteen years old'. This is partly to save tedious repetition of the phrase 'children and teenagers'. It also acts as a reminder that, by law, any person under the age of eighteen is a child. To save similar over-use of the phrase 'club, meeting, or Sunday school class', I have often used either 'club' or 'meeting'. For the same reason I have also used 'story' or 'talk' more or less interchangeably, although the style of teaching will vary with the age groups concerned.

Generally speaking, I have referred to Bible passages rather than quote them. Nevertheless, these references have been included in the hope that they will be consulted, rather than ignored!

Readers outside the UK should be aware that the references to child protection legislation, particularly in chapters 13 and 14, relate specifically to the UK, although the principles of child protection outlined in this book are universally relevant.

The gospel—
God's saving power

Most Christians know that 'gospel' means 'good news'. It is such amazing news that it should be given the headline on every newspaper, and interrupt television and radio programmes. Not only is the message wonderful, it also has direct and personal relevance and significance for every man, woman, and child on our planet. It tells of a God whose love is so immense that he did not spare his own Son, but gave him up to suffering and death for the sake of men and women (see Romans 8:32). It tells of One who pours vast goodness and kindness on those who entrust themselves to him. This news becomes even more astounding when we reflect upon what the Bible tells us both about this God and about ourselves. To make sure that we understand it clearly, we will skim through the opening chapters of Paul's letter to the Romans. It would be very helpful to have this Bible passage open and to read the verses to which I shall refer.

What is God like?
In the ancient world, pagan gods were often represented in the form of humans, birds, animals, or even reptiles (1:23). Greek and Roman deities were usually portrayed in human or semi-human fashion. By contrast, in these verses Paul describes the true God as unique and immensely great. Images are worthless and pointless. They can only convey visible qualities, whereas God is *invisible* (1:20).

He is *immortal* (1:23). He has always existed, and there will never be a time when he no longer is. Cartoonists draw him as a kind but frail old man with a white beard, but nothing could be further from the truth: the years, centuries, and millennia of human history leave him unchanged and unchanging. He has *eternal power* (1:20), and is as mighty today as when he made the heavens and the earth. This strength will last, undiminished, for ever.

The so-called gods of paganism were a strange mixture of the human and the divine in character. They experienced human fits of rage and bouts of jealousy, and were easily offended. But their superhuman power made these swings of mood dangerous. They were unpredictable and unreliable. Their anger could flare up in an instant against a worshipper who had shown consistent devotion over many years. By contrast, God's nature is completely *divine* (1:20), in a category all of its own, unmixed with and untainted by human characteristics or behaviour patterns.

How does man see God?

The views held by many children and adults today are remarkably similar to ancient pagan ideas. The Bible elevates God and teaches that man's main duty and purpose in life is to honour and obey him (Ecclesiastes 12:13). By contrast, ancient and modern unbelievers reverse this emphasis, elevating *man* and thinking that God's chief role is to satisfy human needs and wishes. Modern paganism, like that of old, revolves around obtaining divine help for personal prosperity, health, and happiness. It assumes that we deserve his aid, or can make ourselves worthy of it.

Although many unbelievers think that God is greater than man is, they think that his power is nevertheless limited. Events in individual experience or on the international scene are regarded as outside his control or beyond his concern. Like a genie in a lamp, he can apparently be called upon when a crisis appears, but conveniently ignored the rest of the time. Many pray earnestly for help when in trouble, even when the problem is a direct result of their own sin. More often than not, they then happily forget about God if the outcome pleases them. If it does not, they frequently blame him. This attitude can be seen in adults and children alike.

In stark contrast, the Bible describes a God who is majestic and powerful beyond human understanding. Those who prefer to think of him in any lesser way might just as well carve an image out of stone or wood, or cast one from molten metal, and worship it. They have already replaced the true and living Lord with a 'god' of their own imagination.

Even the portrayal of God in statues or pictures is offensive and deeply insulting to him. It replaces the glory of the Almighty with something hideously inferior. Those who make idols do not show God's greatness, they belittle it (1:22–23). The worshipper bows down to something that has been made, rather than to the Maker of all things (1:25).

Much more could be said about God's nature and character. For now we should briefly note that he is fully aware of human sin and is opposed to it (1:18,24,28). Every act that we perform, every word that we speak, every thought that comes to our minds (and is either dismissed or nursed there) is known to him (see Psalm 139:1–4). What we have seen so far about the Lord makes his kindness truly amazing (see Psalm 8:3–4).

Sin

When many people in the West hear the word 'sin' nowadays they think only of marital unfaithfulness or sexual promiscuity, because this is the way in which popular newspapers use it. Others have been brought up to attend church regularly. They hear about sin in public prayers, and sing hymns about Jesus' death for human sin. Yet many of them have little awareness of what sin actually is, or of how serious a thing it is to be a sinner.

So far we have seen that God is very great. He does not change. He sees and knows everything that we do. God is also kind and generous, but we only see the real extent of this when we understand how utterly unworthy we are of such goodness.

THE SINS OF THE NON-RELIGIOUS

In the first three chapters of Romans, Paul describes two categories of people. Many were living mainly for pleasure. The little religion they had was mere superstition, and did not regulate their behaviour. Few pleasures were off-limits to them, and their lifestyles were driven by the desire to enjoy life to the full. But lack of knowledge about God does not excuse such people. Paul explains that they knew in their consciences that there is a God, and that he is very great (1:18–20). Far from this affecting them, however, they suppressed the truth, forcing it deeper and deeper to the backs of their minds and choosing to ignore and forget it. There is no shortage of such people today.

THE SINS OF THE RELIGIOUS

On the other hand, the Jews of Paul's day knew a considerable amount about the true God, and about his law. They had a strong sense of right and wrong, and, as a result, they felt very superior to those who lived a scandalous lifestyle and who had little regard for God. But the apostle argues that apparently respectable and moral people are also sinners. They may not sin in quite the same way, or to the same extent, as others do. But the *essence* of their sins is the same. Can a man who despises someone who commits adultery honestly say that he himself is entirely free from that sin (1:22)? He might never even literally touch a woman who is not his wife, but he may nevertheless commit the act of adultery many times in his imagination (compare Matthew 5:27–28).

Jews living outside Israel would have felt outraged at the immorality that surrounded them. They would have nodded their heads in agreement at Paul's description of 'every kind of wickedness ... murder, strife, deceit and malice' (1:29) as evidence of a depraved mind. But in the same breath, Paul also mentions offences that seem trivial by comparison: slander, boasting, arrogance, and disobedience to parents. According to the apostle's arguments, these also prove that the human heart is wicked, and are as offensive to the Lord as more obvious sins.

Paul admits that it is far better to know about God than to be ignorant of him. But the mere possession of such knowledge does not guarantee his favour. In fact, the more one knows about the Lord's commands, the greater is one's responsibility to keep them (2:17–24; 3:1–3). Far from speaking peace, God's law thunders 'GUILTY!' against men and women everywhere. The religious and moral person has broken it as well as those who have little respect for God (3:19–20). Trying harder in the future cannot make up for past guilt. In any case, all attempts to win the Almighty's favour are doomed to failure. Acts of sin do not make us sinners. We commit sins because we have a sinful nature. Every step forward in pleasing God is followed by a backward step. This is as true of children as it is of adults, and as they grow up this becomes increasingly evident. 'Unrighteousness' (3:10,12) is a part of human makeup. Outside intervention is needed if anybody is to be saved.

ALL HAVE SINNED—AND *ALL* ARE GUILTY

All have sinned, without exception. Again and again in Romans 3, Paul describes sin as universal, repeating 'no one' or 'not even one' several times. The statement in 3:23 therefore includes children. To 'sin' is to break a specific command. To 'fall short' is to miss the required standard. Both terms demonstrate our predicament. We are guilty. Our sinful nature also prevents us from ever succeeding. All are *under* sin' (3:9). Its power dominates us (compare Ephesians 2:3), and it brings the certainty of God's wrath.

Paul seems to offer a ray of hope that those who do good will gain eternal life (2:7,10), but careful reading of his words dashes to the ground any such hopes. Those who do good in God's sight will most certainly win his approval. But no such people exist. Those who know God's law stand condemned by it (3:19). Those who are ignorant of it are condemned even by the scant knowledge of God that they have (2:12). Human sin is summed up in the words 'there is ... no-one who seeks God. All have turned away ...' (3:11–12). Some people turn away from God with visible defiance. Others do so with apparent politeness and respectability. But all men, women, and children turn from him, *and fail to turn to him,* every single day. The same fate awaits all alike: the wrath and punishment of a holy God (1:18; 3:5–6).

The person who refuses to listen to God is like a man who saves up money a little at a time. But instead of money, he is saving up for himself a little more of God's anger each day, gradually accumulating more and more of it. One day the treasure chest will burst open and its entire contents will pour out (2:5–6). The image is a chilling portrayal of the truth that all reap what they sow (Galatians 6:7). Every one of us once acted like this. Day by day we witness others doing so. Some of them sit next to us in our classroom, lecture theatre or office. Some work with us on the shop floor or in the workshop. Others may even attend our children's meetings.

What does God do?
God makes righteousness available to mankind (3:21); this righteousness comes from God himself. The scholar D. B. Knox defines righteousness as 'conformity to law, especially to the law, mind, and will of God' ('Righteousness', *The New Bible Dictionary*, IVP, 1962). It is bestowed upon everybody who trusts in the Lord Jesus Christ. It is not a reward for

achievement or for continuous effort on the part of those who receive it. It is theirs as a free gift simply by believing in Christ (3:22). None who receive it deserves it; righteousness is granted to men and women *despite* what they have done, not because of it.

God *justifies* the person who trusts in his Son (3:26). To 'justify' means 'to declare righteous a person who has been charged with committing an offence'. It is almost beyond belief that God, who sees every secret of our hearts, and who measures everybody against his own law, should declare anybody righteous. We have seen that nobody receives a favourable verdict on the basis of their attempts to keep God's law: they are declared righteous through having faith in Jesus. Justification is awarded 'freely' and 'by his grace' (3:24). These two expressions underline the immense generosity of God towards sinners who do not deserve it, and who never could become worthy of it. The original Greek expression translated '*by* faith' indicates that people are not justified *because* they have faith, but *by means* of faith. It has often been said that faith is like the hand of a beggar as he reaches out to take money that is held out to him. Justification involves a two-way exchange. All the offences of the sinner were laid on Christ and treated as if they were his; Paul graphically expresses this as Christ being 'made sin for us'. In return, sinners receive Christ's own righteousness (2 Corinthians 5:21). Not only have their sins been forgiven, but they also have a positive righteousness credited to them.

Justification is based on the *redemption* that came through the Lord Jesus (3:24). 'Redemption' is particularly associated with God's deliverance of Israel from Egypt, recorded especially in Exodus 12, when the Lord *set the Israelites free through the payment of a price*. The Israelites were powerless *slaves* to the Egyptians, unable to break free. The time came when God declared a curse on the whole land, and the life of the oldest child of every family was to be taken, including the families of his own people. The Israelite firstborn therefore needed to be set free from the *sentence of death* that God had pronounced, as well as from slavery.

The Lord himself provided a way of escape for his people. Soon they were liberated from their Egyptian overlords, and the Israelite firstborn were also spared death at the hand of the destroying angel. Each family killed a lamb; its death counted as if it was the death of the firstborn child.

God's justice was satisfied, for a life had been taken. But the condemned were spared.

Similarly, Christ's death was a sacrifice (3:25). He died a violent death as a substitute, taking the place of others. The cross was not a great tragedy that consisted in the execution of an innocent man. There God laid upon his own Son the sins of guilty people like you and I, and punished him as if those sins were his own. The judgement that by rights should fall upon the sinner fell instead upon Christ, just as in Old Testament sacrifices the deathblow fell upon an innocent animal instead of upon God's people.

The cross of Christ not only sets us free from the punishment that our sins deserve, it also frees us from the domination of sin. Just as the Israelites were slaves to the will of their Egyptian masters, so the unbeliever is in the grip of sin. Not every person is as bad as he or she could possibly be, but the entire personality of every man and woman is affected and dominated by sin (see Ephesians 2:1–3; Romans 6). God has provided a way for men, women, and children to be freed both from sin's dominating power and from its penalty by the payment of a price. The price could not have been higher. It was the death of his own Son.

The gospel and us

Our guilt makes God's free offer of salvation truly astounding. Instead of the punishment that they deserve, sinners may receive full and free pardon for their sins. They also gain a right standing with God, and numerous other blessings, if they will only believe upon Christ to save them. These things are almost too good to be true. The Christian only dares to believe them because they are written in the Bible.

These truths are not academic. I must ask whether you have seen what God is really like, and that it is impossible to win his favour for yourself. You must make sure that your trust is solely and completely in the Lord Jesus, and that you are not relying at all on what you do or on what you hope to achieve in the future. Too much is at stake simply to hope or assume that all is well between you and God. If you are uncertain at the moment whether or not you have responded to the saving message of Christ, you are certainly in no position to teach others.

However, if we are God's children, we can have great confidence as we seek to share this gospel. Sometimes we will become discouraged, or our enthusiasm will waver for other reasons. But the astonishing news that 'Christ Jesus came into the world to save sinners' (1 Timothy 1:15) is not just a message to tell to others. It is the very means by which God converts people (Romans 1:16). The gospel itself has the power to change the hearts and lives of men, women, and children. Whenever we speak about the Lord, there is the thrilling possibility that somebody will believe and be saved. We must persevere in sharing his Word, and plead with him to bring its power to bear upon some of those to whom we speak.

The message of salvation through the Lord Jesus should also be our delight. The more we appreciate the love of God, the more willing we will be to share it with others. A sense of profound gratitude to the Saviour will help to prevent serving him from being a chore. Along with giving us a sense of privilege in being able to tell others about him, it will help us to keep difficulties and discouragement in perspective.

Paul was overwhelmed by the immense kindness of God through Christ. It made his service for Jesus wholehearted (1:9) and was the great driving force behind his ministry (2 Corinthians 5:14). To Paul, salvation was so wonderful, and Christ so lovely, that it would be terrible if he should ever *not* preach the gospel (1 Corinthians 9:16). Sometimes our hearts are lukewarm. We are afraid of what others will think if we speak about Christ. We easily become discouraged, too. Perhaps these things would happen less often if we meditated more on the vastness of God's goodness to us through the Lord Jesus Christ.

The gospel for children

Children have within them the seeds of the same sins that adults display. They are born with a sinful nature that seeks to go its own way. They do not necessarily commit outrageous sins, and many of them will hopefully not do so in the future. But they are sinners who need to be saved. The gospel will need to be simply and carefully explained to them. But it is the gospel, not Bible stories taught in a sentimental or matter-of-fact way, that they need to hear.

Children must also be able to see the gospel lived out in our lives. Our behaviour, attitudes, and reactions while we are with them will either cause them to think well of the gospel, or make them feel that it has no value or relevance. We will also need to give careful thought to how we can explain God's saving message to children and teenagers. We will consider this in subsequent chapters.

Summary

- The gospel has the power to change the hearts and lives of men, women, and children.
- Whenever we speak about the Lord, there is the thrilling possibility that somebody will believe and be saved.
- Persevere in sharing God's Word, and plead with him to bring its power to bear upon some of those to whom we speak.

Understanding children today

We smile at the person who says that the trouble with going abroad is that there are too many foreigners! There are times, though, when those who work with children feel exasperated with children for this reason: children are so immature!

If we do not understand how children's minds work, we will be very impatient with them, and our attempts to share the gospel with them will be ineffective. Discouragement and even disillusionment will also creep up on us if we expect children to behave like miniature adults.

What are the challenges faced by those involved in children's work today?

Attention

Children cannot sit still or concentrate for as long as adults can. In fact, despite the high standard of education in Britain, the attention span of children seems to be decreasing. A growing number of children underperform in schools, not because they are stupid, but because they are restless and unwilling, or unable, to concentrate. In our meetings their minds will wander if our Bible story lasts too long, if they find it boring, or if the speaker's voice is monotonous.

In school, children do not learn simply by sitting and listening to somebody speaking. They also take in information by means of pictures, and by interaction with teachers and with one another. Older children also learn effectively by reading and thinking for themselves. When you explain a Bible passage, bear this in mind. Ask questions as you proceed, or show visual aids. Craft activities could be devised that are based on the passage taught, or a simple take-home activity sheet could be produced. These would underline the teaching that the children receive.

We are sometimes disappointed when children cannot remember the previous week's Bible story. Sometimes, though, we ourselves have listened with them and are also unable to remember it the following week! Although this may be due to lack of attention when God's Word was being explained, it may simply be the case that it has been crowded out by the routine of a busy week.

Distractions

Some adult Christians will always look around in a church service whenever one or two people arrive late, or even when faint noises occur during the sermon, but remember: the concentration of children is far more fragile. We should keep noise and other disturbances to a minimum while the Scriptures are being explained. Where possible, as many adults as possible should be present throughout the Bible talk, seated among the children so that they are more easily controlled. Any tidying up or other task that needs to be done at this point should be confined to other rooms, and should be carried out as quietly as possible, and by the smallest number of workers that can do it. It is unfair to be disappointed with the children's level of concentration when we ourselves have broken it.

A friend told me that once, while he was preaching, he noticed that a number of people in the congregation were stifling chuckles of laughter. This concerned and surprised him, as they normally listened attentively. After a few minutes, however, he noticed that a large moth that had been fluttering around the chapel had perched on his shoulder without him even noticing. The incident was unfortunate, and lessened the impact of the sermon. Nevertheless, the amusement of the congregation was genuine, not a sign of disrespect for his preaching, or an attempt to distract others. Many of us can probably recall an incident where something amused us when we were expected to be quiet and serious; somehow, the strain of not being able to laugh made it all the harder to contain.

We should always be concerned if children begin to laugh or be silly when God's Word is being explained. Sometimes it is done deliberately, but at other times it is done without malice. We must always discourage it—but we must not automatically assume that it is a sign of disrespect for the gospel of Christ. If something genuinely unusual happens, pause for a moment, acknowledge it with a smile, then recommence.

Immaturity

Many children love to chase one another, pull one another about and play-fight. They take little notice when we urge them to calm down. They do not stop to consider that one of them may get hurt or that parents may blame us for any injuries that occur. Remember that they are children: they simply do not think like adults. Although we need to be firm, we must patiently explain why we are asking them to act, or not to act, in a certain way. In chapter 10 we will consider some methods by which boisterous behaviour can be controlled or channelled.

Bad behaviour

We must try to be kind, fair, and patient, even when children deliberately misbehave. Firstly, the Lord himself is patient and good even to the undeserving, and we are commanded to be the same (Matthew 5:44–48). Secondly, although the Bible insists that everybody is accountable for his or her behaviour, it also recognizes the effect that the influence of others can have. Many in Israel and Judah turned to idol worship because their kings actively promoted and encouraged it (e.g. 1 Kings 15:30,34; 16:30). Children's behaviour (whether good, bad, or average) is largely the product of their upbringing, and each child is a window into his or her family life. As we get to know them and learn about their family lives, we may even be surprised that some of those who attend our meetings are actually as well-behaved as they are.

Dealing with adolescents is particularly challenging. Teenagers are experiencing hormonal changes that affect their moods, fuel their interest in the opposite sex, and encourage them to challenge authority. They are also bigger and stronger than teenagers were twenty or thirty years ago. Some have little idea of their size and strength, while others consciously seek to exploit both. Recent years have produced increasing numbers of teenagers with aggressive tendencies, and this trend is beginning to appear in some younger children. It may be the case that this over-excitability or aggression is partly due to chemicals contained in foods; in some, it may be caused by a lack of discipline, a short attention span, or instability in the home. It may, of course, arise from a combination of these factors. In a small number of cases, it may even be caused by abuse.

Understanding

Children, particularly those of primary school age, do not understand many of the words that adults use, and cannot follow long sentences. Many biblical words, even some that seem very basic to us, will mean little or nothing to children from non-Christian families. If your church uses the Authorized Version of the Bible, it may be worth considering using a more modern version with children. The New King James Version may be an acceptable compromise. Essentially this is the Authorized Version without the use of the older words like 'thee', or 'thou', or word endings such as 'giv*eth*'. If your church has strong views on versions of the Bible, you should check with church officers before using a different one in a club or meeting.

In the 1960s, Sunday school attendance was fairly common. Many parents who did not go to church themselves still encouraged their children to attend Sunday school. Today, many parents who do not go to church themselves are still willing to allow their children to go to Sunday school, but few actively encourage them to do so. At the same time, there is less and less Bible teaching in religious education in schools. This means that, as well as being unfamiliar with some quite common Bible words, many children are also unfamiliar with the basic truths, characters, and stories that the Bible contains. We will need to explain many of the things that we teach.

Worldly wisdom

A large number of children today are left to occupy themselves for much of the time. Both adults in the house may work, or be too busy to bother much with the children. Some may belong to single-parent families. Televisions are left on for long periods of time in many homes and bombard children's minds with much that is wrong. Because of their age, they are unable to think through some of the things that they see and hear, and are easily influenced by them. Some children have a television in their own room and nobody supervises what they watch. Other children access material on DVDs, computer games, or internet sites that is unwholesome and, in some cases, potentially harmful.

Those of us who own televisions can easily become immune to images and storylines that would have shocked us a number of years ago. We should be careful what we ourselves watch, and switch off the television or change channel when the need arises. If you do not have a television, you should consider obtaining a television guide from time to time, and skimming through it. You will probably be shocked even at some of the material screened in the early evening, but at least you will be aware of what some children lap up on a daily basis. I suspect that television has a much stronger influence on behaviour (including our own) than we realize. While children encounter bad influences from many sources, television provides many examples of people who swear almost constantly and of adolescents who frequently scream at their parents. Programmes screened well before nine o'clock in the evening portray experimenting with sex and alcohol as normal and exciting. Although there is little sexually explicit material at this time of day, there are plenty of sordid details in dramas and soaps that can arouse the curiosity or desires of young people.

Sensitivity and vulnerability

Despite some of the images that confront them on television or computer screens, some children have a vivid imagination and can be easily upset or frightened. We must never change the content of the gospel as we share it with them, but we need to be careful not to press some issues too far. For example, although the wrath of God against sin is part and parcel of our message, it would be inappropriate to describe it in lengthy and graphic detail while speaking to children.

Children can also be very open to suggestion. Even without meaning to we can get them to say things by the mere power of persuasion or by the strength of our personality. Care should be taken when explaining the need to respond to the claims of the Lord Jesus. Pressurizing children into saying that they have become Christians is wrong and potentially damaging. Some may go along with what we say, only to become confused and disillusioned some time later. We must learn to explain Christ to them, point them to Christ, and ask Christ to draw them to himself.

Some children say the kind of thing that we want to hear because they are keen to gain our approval. For example, a girl with this tendency may tell us that she reads the Bible and prays every day. It may well be true. We should certainly pray that such things will happen and not be unduly sceptical when they seem to occur. On the other hand, we need to exercise some discernment, especially if we know that the child in question tends to crave approval.

If we are unsure about what we are told, we should not make it obvious. The girl may be telling the truth, and will be hurt and discouraged if she suspects that we do not believe her. We could encourage and help her to read the Scriptures, whether or not she is actually doing so. We could say, for example, 'I'm glad that you say you are reading the Bible at home. It is so important that we get to know the Lord Jesus and learn to love him and trust him. One of the Gospels is a good part of the Bible to read. Shall I show you where to find them?' We could even produce simple activity sheets based on a Bible passage for children to complete if they want to.

The need for tact

Many children have unhappy or unstable home lives. A growing number of children visit their fathers at the weekend. Some homes see a succession of men living with the mother of a family of several children. A family of four or five children may have three or four different fathers. This is a sad situation, but the children have not created it, nor are they responsible for it. Passages of the Bible that touch on family life (such as a series on the Ten Commandments) might be best avoided, but if they do form part of our syllabus, we should deal with them very carefully.

It is easy to embarrass children without meaning to. I remember once asking a fourteen-year-old boy what he got for Christmas. I wish I had not done so, as his main present consisted of underwear and socks. It may be better to ask questions like 'Does your dad work?' rather than 'What work does your dad do?' which carries an assumption that may be wrong.

Nevertheless, we should not be so afraid of embarrassing the children that we avoid chatting to them. Taking an interest in them, even in those who behave badly, is an important way of demonstrating the love of Christ to them. Getting to know them individually will help us to avoid questions that they will find awkward. It will also help to build a rapport with them, and to earn their respect.

Changing times?

Comment has already been made upon the increase in behavioural problems among children and teenagers. Nowadays, too, parents have higher expectations of individuals and organizations that educate or entertain their children, and will expect answers if anything goes wrong. Both of these trends are likely to continue, and will be further addressed in later chapters.

Other developments may soon affect our attempts to tell others about Christ. British society is increasingly concerned with the concept of toleration. We are all being urged to respect the views of others and to recognize and uphold diversity in society. Much of this stems from a genuine desire to protect minority groups against being victimized; however there are unhelpful elements in this modern drive for toleration.

All kinds of lifestyles and views are permitted, even promoted. Those who claim that, from a moral point of view, certain things are right and others wrong are viewed with suspicion and antagonism. During 2005 there were several occasions when the police questioned individuals about 'homophobic' incidents. The individuals concerned had simply made comments against homosexual practice or expressed concern about displays of gay literature. These incidents are isolated, but it should concern us that police involvement even took place. Evangelicals in Britain have often been accused of being intolerant. Now they are beginning to be portrayed as antisocial. These trends are at an early stage of development, but they are growing. The foundation stone of the gospel is the existence of a God who is morally pure and who has absolute standards of right and wrong. Churches that uphold the biblical message will be viewed with increasing suspicion, even hostility, and a growing number of parents may be reluctant to allow their children to attend Christian clubs and meetings.

A similar situation is unfolding regarding religious beliefs. For many centuries Britain has practised religious toleration. Now, though, the claim that salvation can only be found in Jesus is considered insulting to people of other faiths. Some who advocate toleration think that such views should not be expressed openly. Biblical truth is beginning to be seen as a threat to harmony in society. I heard recently of a pastor who was approached by the police as a result of handing out evangelistic tracts in an area where many Muslims live. No action resulted (for no crime had been committed), but it is an indication of how times are changing in twenty-first century Britain.

For many years Gideons International have been permitted to distribute Bibles in schools and to place them in hospitals and hotels. A small but increasing number of institutions are now withdrawing that permission on the grounds that people of other faiths may be offended, and are requesting that the Bibles be collected and taken away. It is only fair to say that much of this pressure is not coming from people of other faiths who feel insulted. It is being brought to bear by others who fear that these people *may* take offence. In some cases, this 'political correctness' may simply be an excuse for atheists in positions of authority to exclude Christian influence.

The voice of church denominations is also more broad-minded than it used to be. This is seen in its acceptance of sins and lifestyles to which God is opposed. Increasingly, too, church leaders are teaching that all religious faiths are routes that lead to heaven. Any who stand and speak clearly for biblical truth are becoming more and more isolated. They are being portrayed as on the fringe of Christianity, not as representing authentic Christian faith.

These pressures are likely to have considerable impact upon attempts to spread the gospel in the near future. It is quite probable that attempts to win *children* for Christ will be viewed with particular suspicion and concern. At the moment we have enormous freedom of speech to explain God's saving message to lost sinners of all ages. We do not know how long we will have such liberty, and should take full advantage of it while we can.

Summary

• Remember, children are children! Don't expect them to behave like miniature adults. They cannot sit still or concentrate for as long as adults can.
• Try to be kind, fair, and patient, even when children deliberately misbehave.
• Many children are unfamiliar with the basic truths, characters, and stories that the Bible contains. We must explain the things that we teach.
• Many children have unhappy or unstable home lives.

- We should take full advantage of the freedom we have to win children for Christ while we can.

Planning a syllabus

If you help to run a midweek children's meeting, you may feel slightly envious of Sunday school teachers. They probably have a structured series of lessons (a syllabus), and an outline of each week's story. Their material may contain accompanying visual aids and activity sheets. The lessons cover a wide range of subject matter from Old and New Testaments, possibly with occasional topical studies. However, there is no reason why you should not plan a syllabus for your midweek meeting, and this chapter is designed to help give you ideas and get you started.

If you are a Sunday school teacher, it may be worth evaluating the material that you use. Perhaps there are some parts or themes of the Bible that never seem to be covered, but that could usefully be explained to the children in your care. Perhaps there is other material that you could use from time to time, or maybe you could even devise your own. Some useful resources are listed in Appendix 1. It is also worth remembering that a book designed for use with younger children can often be adapted for teenagers.

Where to start

There are several ways of producing a series of lessons. You could browse through some of the teaching aids available, and copy or adapt a syllabus from them. Alternatively, you might decide to teach a specific part of the Bible without such material. You would need to split it into a number of portions for the individual talks or stories. You might even feel that it would be useful to cover certain themes; if you find it difficult to think of suitable passages for these, your pastor or another mature believer may be able to help.

It is best to restrict a series of talks to ten or twelve at the very most before moving to another. This will help to maintain interest (or at least to prevent undue boredom!) and will enable a variety of Bible passages and themes to be covered. Sections of the Scriptures that describe people and events are usually the easiest to teach. As far as possible, keep matters simple. If you wish children to understand about the sacrificial death of

Christ, it is probably best to teach from one of the Gospel accounts. This will be much easier for them to understand than a detailed description of Old Testament sacrifices. You could also refer to some of the explanations contained in the letters of Paul (or, possibly, Peter, as one of Christ's close friends and an eyewitness of the Lord's death). I do not wish to imply that we should never seek to speak about Old Testament animal sacrifices; nevertheless, too many attempts to find Christ in all the Scriptures may well confuse children.

Character studies

A little imagination can produce a 'slant' that can make a passage fresher to us and, in turn, to the children. Children often relate well to Bible characters. A helpful series could be based on the life of Simon Peter. It could begin with how he became a follower of the Lord Jesus, and go on to some of the remarkable things that he heard the Saviour say and do. It could include some of Peter's highs and lows. One talk could focus on the occasion when he walked on the water (then sank, and was rescued by the Lord). Another could describe the Lord's transfiguration from Peter's standpoint. You could consider his proud boast that he would remain faithful to his Master even if no others did, and his bitter tears when he denied him not once, but three times. You could hone in on his intense sadness on his way to the tomb on the Sunday morning, and his amazement when he got there. The next obvious step would be his restoration, and you could include the touching words to the women: 'Tell his disciples *and Peter*' (Mark 16:7—probably intended as 'especially to Peter, in view of his particular sorrow and sense of guilt'). You could follow him through the early chapters of Acts, and end by explaining that he was probably killed because of his faith. Bringing together these incidents and teaching them from Peter's point of view can give them an added impact, even if they are familiar to some of the children.

Another syllabus could be based on different characters with a common theme, such as people who met the Lord Jesus, or some of the many kings described in the Bible; some of these kings ruled over God's people, others were foreign; some are remarkable for their godliness, others stand out as warnings. Ones that may come to mind are the Pharaoh encountered by

Moses, kings Ahab, Manasseh, Josiah, Jehoiakim, and Belshazzar, or the various New Testament kings who were each called Herod.

Pharaoh (Exodus 5–14) could be considered as 'A king who kept changing his mind'. Like many people today he cried to God for help, then turned his back on him. He made repeated promises to change, but never did. Many children are fascinated by those who break sporting or other records: Ahab (1 Kings 17–22) was 'A king who broke all the records—*for sin*!' Despite a godly upbringing, Manasseh was 'A king who went off the rails' (2 Kings 21; 2 Chronicles 33); his story is especially relevant to children with Christian parents. The clear repentance that he displayed later is hugely encouraging, proving that nobody's sin puts him or her beyond the reach of God's grace. His repentance is also sobering, for he was only partly successful in his genuine efforts to undo the harm he had done earlier. In contrast, Josiah (despite an *un*godly upbringing) proved to be 'A king who loved God's book' (2 Kings 22–23; 2 Chronicles 34–35). Jehoiakim (Jeremiah 36; 2 Kings 23–24; 2 Chronicles 36) was 'A king who threw God's book on the fire'; like him, many people today refuse to listen to the parts of God's Word that they do not like, and only take note of the parts that please them. Belshazzar was 'A king who pushed God too far', especially in view of his knowledge of God's dealings with Nebuchadnezzar (Daniel 1–5). Many people today do not like Jesus as he *really* is and, deep down, wish that he had never come. With this in mind, the Herod spoken of in the infancy of Christ was 'A king who wanted to get rid of Jesus' (Matthew 2). The Herod who examined our Lord after his arrest was 'A king who was curious about Christ', or 'A king who wanted a different kind of Jesus'. He longed to see a miracle but refused to accept the Saviour's claims (Luke 23:6–12). A series along these lines could strike a number of important chords, especially with teenagers.

Other possible themes

A syllabus for teenagers could even be based on a particular word. A good concordance is worth buying. It is basically a list of Bible words, and under each word there is a list of passages where it occurs. A concordance would help you to locate specific verses, or to find verses related to ones that you know.

You could examine some of the 'if' passages of the New Testament. The verses beginning 'If anyone would come after me ...' (Matthew 16:24ff.), explain what it means to be a real Christian. You could consider 'If God is for us, who can be against us?' (Romans 8:31—but if God is *against* us, who can be *for* us?!) and, 'If anyone is in Christ ...' (2 Corinthians 5:17). The apostle John holds out a promise: 'If we confess our sins ...' (1 John 1:9—but if we *do not* confess our sins, we have no claim to the promise). If the group contains believers, you could focus on: 'If you then were raised with Christ ...' (Colossians 3:1ff., NKJV). Alternatively, a series of talks could be based on basic Bible truths or, for older children, 'apologetics' (biblical answers to the kind of questions often asked by unbelievers). Remember, though, that Bible talks should go beyond merely explaining biblical truth or trying to correct wrong ideas. Whenever we explain Bible teaching or seek to confront false beliefs, we must always move on to show what these things mean *for our hearers*.

If you teach in Sunday school, a large proportion of the children in your class may come from Christian homes and be fairly familiar with the Bible. This may allow you to teach parts of the Scriptures that other children might find difficult to understand. If you have a computer, you could try to devise simple activity sheets, with puzzles or pictures to colour. Crosswords or word searches are quite easy to produce using a word processing or spreadsheet program. I have occasionally produced an overview of a whole book of the Bible that my teenage class has worked through over two or three weeks. Teenagers in Sunday school may benefit from a bird's-eye view of Bible history, or an occasional look at a topic such as archaeology and the Bible. A particular series in your teaching material may present an opportunity to consider a condensed Christian biography in several brief episodes of a few minutes each week. For example, if your material deals with the book of Romans, you could produce a brief, serialized account of the life of Martin Luther. This would give the children a grasp of theology and church history, as well as furnish them with a stirring role model. Other church members may be able to suggest ideas or help to produce material.

A main lesson aim

If you are responsible for producing the syllabus for the talks, you could go beyond simply producing a rota of speakers along with the relevant Bible passage. Any who are inexperienced at teaching children will value some additional help. So, too, might some who do not help regularly with the club, but who speak at it occasionally. Unless you inform them, they will have no idea what has been covered in previous weeks, nor what is due to be explained on future occasions. A series of Bible talks can sound remarkably similar week after week, even though the Scripture passages are different! This can happen even if published material is used as a basis for the stories. A friend once told me that the Sunday school lessons he used for primary children often seemed to consist of the need to trust Jesus and not be afraid of the dark! Alternatively, so many details or practical lessons can be packed into the talk that there is no time to focus upon any individual lesson that the children need to take to heart.

Along with the syllabus, therefore, it's a good idea to suggest one main teaching aim for each particular week. This would help to avoid repetition that loses the children's interest, and would help to ensure that a range of the Bible's teaching and challenges is presented. It would also provide a structure and focus for those who prepare the talks, and help them to explain to the children how they should respond to the passage that is being taught.

The account of Zacchaeus (Luke 19) is full of lessons, probably too many to mention adequately when explaining it to children. Depending on other passages in the series of studies, it could be used in one of several ways. Zacchaeus is the proof that wealth is not everything, and that Christ alone can satisfy our hearts. After all, Zacchaeus was not a victim of society, ignored and hated by those who should have taken pity on him: he exploited others to build up his own wealth. Alternatively, your main emphasis could be upon the compassion of Christ for great sinners. The account of Zacchaeus is a marvellous example, too, of what it means to become a follower of the Lord Jesus Christ. A drastic change came over the man, and he took actual, specific actions to make amends for the wrongs he had done.

Your time is limited; so is the attention span of the children. If you try to cram in too much, you will have to rush through your material, and risk losing some of the impact of the story. Focusing on one point in particular will allow you the time to develop it, and will help the children to remember it, too.

Providing further help

When compiling the syllabus, you could also provide a brief summary, perhaps consisting of just a few paragraphs, for those who will teach. If the passage includes a lot of detail, you could offer suggestions on what to include and what to leave out. You could suggest a memory verse, and a possible way to introduce the talk. You could also highlight possible difficulties and ways to deal with them. For example, if the syllabus includes one of the miraculous healings performed by Christ, it is important that the impression is not given that Jesus *always* heals the sick.

I have found that those who tell the Bible stories usually appreciate such guidance, provided that it is stressed that it is intended as a *suggested* outline, and not a blueprint that must be slavishly followed. Those who teach should feel free to adapt it, and to include their own material. They should also feel that their leader trusts their ability to do so.

The provision of additional guidelines will create extra work for leaders who are already heavily committed, but the benefits to be gained make the effort worthwhile. There may be church members who are unable to help with the actual running of the children's meeting who would be willing to produce some written material for those who do.

Summary

- Restrict a series of talks to ten or twelve at the very most.
- Use your imagination to get a fresh 'slant' on material that may be familiar to the children.
- Plan one main teaching aim for each particular week.
- If possible, provide a brief summary for those who will teach, perhaps suggesting a memory verse, and a way to introduce the talk.

Chapter 3

1 From the account of Elijah (1 Kings 16:29–2 Kings 2:18) devise a syllabus either for six or ten talks (to correspond roughly with the duration of a school term or half-term). Select a main teaching aim for each talk.

2 For *one* of these talks, prepare a brief summary, and find an appropriate memory text. (If necessary, ask other Christians to help.) In the summary, include the main teaching aim. If relevant, mention any details in the passage that may need a little explanation, and highlight any areas where particular care may need to be exercised when delivering the talk, to prevent the children from drawing wrong conclusions.

Preparing the Bible story—making a start

'God has given us a book full of stories ... but the story of Jesus is best.' This hymn that I sang as a child was rather sentimental, but its writer was probably trying to encourage children to read the Bible for themselves. The hymn made the point that the Scriptures do not consist of page after page of academic theology or ethical codes of conduct, but stories. It is helpful for us to remember this, too. Individual events and history are described in considerable detail. Some incidents are described in such detail and so vividly that we almost feel as if we were there ourselves. We can feel the emotions of the characters involved. Sometimes a character's whole life is sketched out from cradle to deathbed. There are tragedies and triumphs. Some passages are exciting and full of suspense. Others, for example, those that describe times when God's people proved unfaithful to him, are quite depressing. There is drama in abundance.

It is most helpful, for example, that the Bible does not simply teach us in an abstract way that we should persevere; instead it gives us some stirring role models who kept going through tougher and more sustained trials than any that we have yet encountered. We are able to see how God stood by them through thick and thin, and we are encouraged to trust him to do the same for us.

When we are teaching narrative passages to children, therefore, we must avoid two mistakes. One is to skim over the events described as quickly as we can and so reduce the episode to a string of lessons that they should take to heart. The other is to concentrate so hard on telling the story vividly that we neglect to show the children what it means *for them today*.

A different kind of story

Children need to understand that Bible stories are *factual accounts*. From time to time we can simply mention this as we prepare to sing or pray with them, or as we begin to teach them. Some weeks, instead of saying, 'Tonight's story is about …' we could say, 'Tonight we are going to find out what happened when …' We can say that God is very great, and easily capable of performing some of the remarkable acts described in his Word.

We should try to avoid saying things that children may misinterpret. If we refer to Goliath, it can be more helpful to say that he was 'huge' or 'very tall' than to describe him as a 'giant', which gives the impression that he was a strange, semi-human creature like those found in fairy tales. Better still, we could check out his height and place a marker on the wall as a visual aid!

At the most profound level, the Scriptures are God's own word. They have been 'breathed out' (a better translation of 'inspired' or 'given by inspiration', 2 Timothy 3:16) by the Almighty. Their purpose is to teach and equip men and women, and boys and girls, for godly living. Throughout our preparation, we need to keep this firmly in our minds. As well as recounting a story, we must also seek to explain how our hearers should respond to its lessons. Given the age of our hearers, we need to be careful how far we press certain matters, but we must keep to our goal of presenting Christ and his salvation to them. For that reason, as we saw in our previous chapter, it is good to have one main teaching lesson to convey to the children.

Putting yourself in the passage

You may have no books or resources at all that will help, or you may have many. You might even have a written outline of the lesson that you are to teach. In the first stages of your preparation, it is helpful to leave all these to one side and to focus only on the Scripture passage itself. You should read it slowly, thoughtfully, a number of times over. You should consider it humbly and prayerfully, for its challenges, warnings, or promises are addressed to you as much as to the children to whom you will speak. Consulting Bible study aids too early can stifle original thinking and result simply in passing on the thoughts of others.

One of the best ways to get to grips with a narrative passage is to try to picture the scene. This needs to be done carefully, otherwise you will substitute your own version of the biblical account for the actual one.

Nevertheless, careful use of imagination can help to overcome overfamiliarity with some passages, and help you to appreciate the impact that the words or events would have had on those who witnessed or took part in them.

It may be helpful to consider as an example the raising to life of Jairus' daughter (Luke 8:40–56). The factual details are straightforward. Putting yourself in the place of Jairus, in the place of the servant who brought the news that it was pointless to bother the Lord any further, or in the shoes of one of the crowd or of one of the disciples, demands a little more time and effort. Doing so will help to bring the passage alive to you, and, in turn, to the children. Another related means of grasping the passage is to ask yourself questions as you read it: 'How might this man have felt when Jesus said to him …?' or 'How might I have felt if I had been in the crowd when Jesus …?'

Study aids

Once you have spent some time thinking through the Scripture itself, you can consult various books and, if you have one, the lesson outline. Good books will make sure that you have understood the passage clearly, clarify details of which you are unsure, and stimulate your thoughts further. They may provide background information on places that are mentioned, or explain customs that were common in Bible times but that seem very strange today.

Commentaries explain the meaning of the text, either verse by verse or section by section. Some are very detailed or quite technical, others are particularly good at pointing out the practical lessons to be learned. Bible dictionaries give valuable information about people, places, and important scriptural words or themes, and give a helpful summary of the contents of each book of the Bible. As well as being useful for preparing Bible talks, we can gain huge personal benefit from browsing through them. Bible atlases often contain useful photographs as well as maps, and will help us to visualize places and events more clearly. Pastors or church members with well-stocked libraries may be willing to recommend and lend books. If you borrow books, remember to take good care of them and return them promptly!

Although helpful, any books or the written outline of the lesson that you are to teach should be used as a reference guide and framework only. You should not feel that you may only say what they contain, or that you must say everything that they teach.

Starting early

It is best to begin to study the passage as early as possible. Several shorter spells of reflection are generally more productive than one mammoth session. Even odd spare moments (even the busiest of us have them!) can be used to think through the passage. Walking about or waiting at the supermarket checkout provides brief but frequent opportunities for turning things over in your mind. The more time you can spend thinking about the story, the more you will feel its force. This will give an added dimension when you speak to the children. It will also benefit your own soul.

There may be times when your circumstances force you to prepare at the last moment, but it is unwise to make this a habit. If you begin several days in advance, and some unexpected demand on your time arises, you will hopefully still find enough time to plan your talk. If, on the other hand, you regularly leave your entire preparation until the evening before you are due to speak, sooner or later some minor crisis will arise on that evening that will leave you with hardly any time at all to study.

You may genuinely struggle to find time to prepare thoroughly, and I would not wish to be critical of anybody whose routine is hugely demanding. If we regularly rush our study, though, it may indicate that we have failed to grasp the seriousness of our task. The children stand in great need of salvation. The Bible is God's own out-breathed word. If we are urging the children to take the Bible seriously when they hear it explained, we should take it equally seriously when we are planning to explain it to them. If genuinely pressed for time, it is important to concentrate fully while studying, thus using to the full the limited time available.

Some sermons that we hear affect us deeply. Very often this happens because the man and his message carry conviction and passion. These lend authority to his words, whether he is declaring a warning, a promise, or a challenge, or describing the greatness of God's love. His sermon hits home partly because he himself is gripped by what he is saying. Men who preach like this do not race through their preparation, but prayerfully meditate on the passage from which they are to preach. They see with fresh eyes the loveliness of Christ or the awfulness and the subtle power of sin. They take delight in a particular promise, or vow to resist sin more seriously as a result of the warnings in the passage. Teaching children is very different from preaching a sermon. Nevertheless, the more we study and meditate upon the Scripture portion that we are seeking to explain, the more likely we will be to speak with true feeling and conviction.

Putting pen to paper

Making notes as you consider the passage will help your concentration, especially if you are tired. Note-making ensures that you will not forget some of the thoughts that come to mind, even if you do not use them all. Writing and redrafting notes will enable you to give adequate time to each part of the talk when you actually come to speak. You should eliminate as many distractions as you can while studying the passage. To prepare while half-watching a favourite television programme is not to take your duty seriously enough.

While preparing, it is helpful to visualize the faces of the children to whom you will speak. This will help you to pitch it at the right level and to choose language that they will understand. Some words or expressions that are part of every Christian's vocabulary may mean little to them, or may carry quite different meanings. To many people, including teenagers, 'sin' often means the sexual scandals that splash the front pages of some newspapers. 'Bless' means little to many, or may suggest sprinkling with 'holy water' or the granting of some mystical power or goodness. You should try to be aware, too, of possible pitfalls. Unless you are careful and discreet, passages like the account of Joseph and Potiphar's wife will result in knowing glances and sniggers (even from quite young children), and will be remembered for all the wrong reasons.

The hidden dimension

To a considerable extent, explaining a Bible passage to children is a skill that can be learned and developed, and we should continually aim to improve our abilities. But there is also a dimension to it that is altogether outside our power and control. We could accumulate years of experience in teaching God's Word to children. Each time, we could spend hours preparing a talk, and present it in a way that regularly holds the children spellbound. They could be emotionally moved by what we say, and it could abide in their memories far into the future. But that is not our aim. In fact, our goal is impossible for us to achieve. We are utterly powerless to bring about a change of heart in any of our listeners. We cannot bring them a single millimetre closer to the kingdom of Christ. They have hearts of stone that are impenetrable to the gospel message.

By contrast, we may feel very unskilled at preparing a Bible talk, and may regularly tell ourselves that, when we have spoken, it appears to have little impact. Yet, even through our limited abilities, a seed may begin to grow quietly and secretly in the hearts of some of the children (Mark 4:26–29). God may use even some of our faltering words to stir their consciences. He alone can bring salvation to them. This should challenge and humble us, and drive us to ask him to do it. But he is also *more than able* to do so; this should encourage us when we lose heart, and give us confidence in our prayers.

Summary

- Start your preparation early.
- At first, focus only on the Scripture passage itself. Make notes as you study.
- Consult Bible commentaries, dictionaries, and atlases.
- Visualize the faces of the children to whom you will speak. This will help you to pitch your talk at the right level and to choose language that they will understand.
- Remember, however experienced we are, God alone can bring salvation to the children.

1 Find words or brief expressions that could be substituted for the following Bible terms:

bless (in the sense of God blessing men and women); heaven; sin; righteousness; repentance.

2 Please make sure that you do this with the Bible passage open before you, to ensure that your 'eye-witness account' is in line with the details contained in the Bible!

Write a brief account of the incident of the paralysed man who was let down through the roof (Mark 2:1–12; Luke 5:17–26) from the point of view of at least two of the following:

(a) a spectator in the house;

(b) one of the friends;

(c) the paralysed man;

(d) one of the teachers of the law.

(Make sure that you include 'your' own reactions and feelings as events unfolded, as well as details of the events themselves!)

Preparing the Bible story— fine-tuning

It's important to be realistic. In a Sunday school class, some children of Christian parents may quite enjoy learning God's Word, but others will be present because their parents insist that they attend. Many, perhaps most, of the children who attend a midweek club come mainly for the games or other activities. As we settle them down, ready for the Bible talk, some of their faces show evidence that they are beginning to switch off, or are looking for things to distract them while it lasts.

The next two or three minutes are crucial. If we can gain their attention now, we may be able to keep it for most of the story. If we fail to secure it at the very start, we are unlikely to do so part-way through. Some preachers are very skilled at arresting the attention of their congregations, and by listening carefully to them we may find ideas that we can copy or adapt.

Arousing curiosity

We have already thought how imagination could help us to speak about the raising of Jairus' daughter (Luke 8:40–56). You could introduce this particular story by focusing on the crowd, perhaps along these lines: 'Some of the crowd, maybe, had come because they wanted to hear some of the marvellous things that Jesus said. Some had come hoping to see him perform a miracle. Some people in the crowd needed a miracle themselves, as they were ill—some of them had been ill for a long time, perhaps even born ill. Perhaps there were some who were blind, and had not been able to see for many years. Maybe they had never seen their children's faces! Some, perhaps, had never walked in their whole lives. But one man needed to see the Lord Jesus more urgently than anybody else did. He did not have much time. His daughter was not just ill, she was dying. If he did not manage to see Jesus soon, it would be too late!'

Sometimes you may be able to bring something along that will help to win the attention of the children as you begin. This approach would become stale if used every week, but most children are easily intrigued as a bag is rustled or as the object inside is slowly pulled free. You could, perhaps, use an item that relates to the very happiest, or very saddest, moment of your life, and proceed with the similar happiness or deep sadness experienced in the story that you are going to tell. You could, for example, introduce the parable of the lost coin by showing the children something that is very precious to you and that you would hate to lose.

Curiosity can be aroused by highlighting common mistakes that people make about biblical truths. You could begin a talk about the coming of the Lord Jesus like this: 'Some people think that Jesus came to teach people—but that isn't the main reason he came. Other people think that he came so that we could copy the ways in which he was kind. But that isn't the real reason that he came, either. Today we are going to learn the *main* reason why he came ...'

Identifying with characters

Some passages present clear opportunities to strike a chord with the children's own experience. You could start the story of Zacchaeus, for example, by reminding the children how frustrating it can be when we are unable to see something important because other people are in the way. You could say something along the lines of, 'Put your hand up if you have ever been in a crowd of people and couldn't see because you were stuck behind a lot of grown-ups!' Then invite some of the children to relate their experiences briefly.

You could introduce the account of Jairus' daughter by telling it from her father's point of view. This would help the children to put themselves in his shoes and grasp the extent of his distress. 'He watched his daughter become ill, then get worse and worse. He tried to make her better, but it was no good. Nobody else knew what to do, either. Soon she was *very* ill. She might even die, even though she was only a child. But ... perhaps Jesus could make her better! With his heart pounding in his chest, he rushed out of the house towards the crowd that had gathered. He began to push his way through. He had to be quick, or it would be too late!'

Ending well

It is important to draw out practical lessons for the children throughout the telling of a Bible story, and not restrict this to the final few moments. Nevertheless, the conclusion of the Bible talk is the particular time when their consciences need to be addressed. The story is not just an interesting tale. It also has a point, something to say to *them,* a lesson to be taken to heart. In a sense, everything that has been explained so far has been building up to this point.

Unless you give some specific thought to it in advance, your conclusion will probably just fizzle out. You might fumble for words. You might find you say a sentence that is intended to be your final one, but it will not sound quite right. Perhaps you will try to say it a little more clearly or forcefully, but it still lacks something. It's easy to become frustrated trying to invent a grand finale on the spur of the moment! In the end you will probably be forced to admit defeat, and mumble a last half-hearted sentence. What was intended to stir and to challenge your hearers' minds has fallen flat. You have lost much of the impact that your message could have had.

The conclusion of your talk will vary with the passage under consideration, and the amount of force that you lend it will depend partly on the age of the children. But it should be fairly direct, concise, and unambiguous. It is no use finishing the story of Jairus' daughter simply by saying, 'Well! There's a lot for us to learn from that story, isn't there? Now let's pray …' You need to explain precisely *what* should be learned from it. If you are teaching children of primary school age, your ending could be along these lines: 'Sometimes we feel like Jairus. We want to trust the Lord Jesus, but some of our friends, or even grown-ups whom we know, tell us that there is no point! And, like Jairus, we sometimes wonder whether they are right, and whether it really *is* silly to trust in the Lord Jesus. But Jairus did not give up! He listened to what Jesus said rather than to what everyone else said. He found out for himself that Jesus really can be trusted. He was so glad that he had trusted him, and, if we really trust the Lord Jesus for ourselves, we will be, too!'

However you end, it is important to plan it in advance. You should also have the confidence to stick to your planned conclusion, especially if you have not given many talks before, and resist the temptation to try to improve upon it while you are actually speaking.

Editing the material

Read through your notes and be prepared to alter them. You should ask yourself whether the children will understand the words and phrases that you have used. It may be better to find simpler words and expressions. There may be times when you decide to keep your original choice of vocabulary but include a brief explanation. Perhaps your notes contain the same words over and over again. If so, try to find others that have the same meaning, in order to give some variety to what you say.

If you are fairly new to teaching children, it is helpful to practise your talk by reading it to yourself aloud; if this makes you feel self-conscious, you can always read it in a whisper! While you do this you should keep an eye on the clock or on your watch. Perhaps you wonder what the point of doing this is, and why it is not enough just to read through your notes silently?

Most of us can read quicker than we can speak. If you simply read your notes silently and to yourself, you will get a false idea of how long your story will last. If it seems to last for about the right amount of time when you read it *through*, it will almost certainly last too long when you actually tell the story to the children.

As a general rule, it is better for a talk to be slightly shorter than normal, rather than longer—this will help to keep the children's interest. I tend to be long-winded. Sometimes this is because I have too much material, and I have not been disciplined enough to leave out some detail from the passage. More usually I find that additional thoughts come to me as I speak. I say things that were not in my notes at all, or speak a little longer about things that I intended to mention briefly. However hard I try, I find it very difficult to stick to what I have written down! My solution is to set myself a slightly shorter deadline for teaching the children than I really need. If the Bible talk usually lasts for between ten and fifteen minutes, I aim to speak for ten. I will probably actually speak for about twelve or thirteen minutes, but my talk will still be within reasonable bounds. On the other hand, if I aim to talk for the *maximum* normal time of fifteen minutes, I will probably speak for nearly twenty, and lose the children's interest.

Ensuring reverence for God's Word

We should not make the Bible passage that we are teaching sound silly or trivial by using humour or gimmickry. Examples of preaching that are recorded in the Bible use humour to a limited extent and in a careful way. Quite often sarcasm or irony is employed to make a point (such as Isaiah 44:12–20), or we read things that make us smile, but we rarely encounter material in the Scriptures that makes us laugh out loud. The biblical pattern should make us keep humour under careful control when explaining God's Word.

I have occasionally heard preachers explain a passage of Scripture almost as a hilarious or far-fetched tale. I hope that they have done this from a genuine desire to 'connect' with the hearer. However, I sometimes suspect that the man in question has done it because he enjoys the reaction that he receives. If we truly believe that the Bible is God's own word, we should treat it seriously and with respect. If we encourage children or teenagers to laugh at it one minute, they are unlikely to believe its saving message the next.

It is easy to make a passage sound trivial or silly out of a sincere attempt to be contemporary. When telling the story of Esther, for example, it may be useful to say something like, 'If it happened nowadays, one of the king's officials would have used the telephone to pass on the king's message to gather together all the beautiful young ladies.' I am not convinced that it is helpful to say (as I once heard), 'One of the king's officials got on the telephone to get all the beauties together.'

Summary

- Plan to catch the children's attention at the beginning: if you can gain their attention now, you may be able to keep it for most of the story.
- Plan your conclusion in advance, and stick to it. Explain *what* should be learned from the story.
- Check the language level of your talk—will you be understood?

- Time yourself reading your talk out loud—aim for it to be slightly shorter than normal.
- Is your talk reverent? If we encourage children or teenagers to laugh at God's Word one minute, they are unlikely to believe its saving message the next.

1 Write a brief introduction and a conclusion (with practical lessons for the children!) for the incident of the paralysed man (Mark 2:1–12; Luke 5:17–26) and for the account of David's meeting with Goliath (1 Samuel 17).

2 Below, three Bible references are listed. For the passage in Acts, and for *one* of the passages from Luke, make brief notes on:

(a)   how the 'talk' or sermon began;

(b)   why the beginning of the talk was effective;

(c)   which features in the content or style of the whole address made it easy for the original hearers to understand;

(d)   how the sermon or address ended, along with your observations on what made the conclusion effective.

Luke 12:13–21; Luke 15; Acts 17:16–34

(Some people think that in Acts 17 Paul preached in a radically different style from his normal one, and that, unhappy with the relative lack of success, he never preached in that style again. Paul's different approach, however, is easily explained by the non-Jewish nature of his hearers. They would have been baffled by a lengthy exposition of the Old Testament, with which they would have been entirely unfamiliar. Paul's apparent lack of success also needs to be carefully reconsidered, given the conversion of several hearers; but even the apostle did not enjoy unlimited success when he preached the gospel, as other passages of Acts clearly demonstrate. Acts 17 has therefore been included here as a helpful example of an effective address.)

Making it visual

S ome people are very lively when they are speaking, even in personal conversation. They wave their arms, shrug their shoulders, and point their fingers. Their eyebrows rise and fall, and they pull many and varied facial expressions. They quiver dramatically as they recount something frightening. If they are telling us about some back pain that they have endured, they may stoop, wince, and put a hand on their back. Listening to them can be an intense and tiring experience!

Gestures and facial expressions

When giving a children's talk, it is best not to try to mimic other people, or turn Bible stories into amateur dramatic performances. Too many instances of face pulling, or even a few instances of pulling exaggerated faces, will make you look ridiculous and destroy the impact of the passage that you are teaching. So, too, will a large number of body actions. But a few subtle gestures or facial expressions can help to make a story more dramatic. For example, if you are recounting how Moses hid his face when the Lord God spoke to him from the burning bush (Exodus 3:6), you too could put on a frightened expression, look to one side, and put your hands in front of your face.

Visual aids

You might want to show pictures to help the children to visualize the story that you are teaching—perhaps an artist's impression of the events that you are describing. Some Sunday school materials include large pictures, or images on a CD, for this specific purpose. These are often very simple illustrations that consist mainly of outlines with very little detail. They are bold, clear, and easy for children to take in. You could hold up one at a time as the story unfolds, or you could attach them to the wall. For older children you might be able to use diagrams, charts, or maps. With some searching you should be able to find Bible study aids and useful clip-art images on CDs produced by Christian publishers or other organizations, to use as you tell the story. Some suppliers are mentioned in Appendix 1.

You may be able to hold up a book while you speak so that the children can see the picture. By definition, a visual aid needs to be easy to see, and any pictures that are indistinct or too small for the children to see clearly are best avoided. Test a picture's suitability in advance by propping up the book on a table and viewing it from a few yards away.

Your church (or one of its members) may have a laptop computer and digital projector, or an overhead projector, that you could use to project pictures as you tell the Bible story. These devices also offer a useful way of enlarging pictures and transferring them to paper for visual aids or for painting activities. If using an overhead projector, first trace a picture onto an acetate sheet. At this stage, you can leave out some detail in order to simplify the picture and so make it clearer. Then project the image onto a large piece of paper temporarily fixed to a wall. The distance between the projector and the wall will determine the degree of enlargement. Now ink-in the outline onto the paper. The process is, of course, quicker and easier with a projector connected to a computer. Clip-art images, graphic files from commercially produced CDs, or scanned images can also be projected onto paper attached to a wall.

Once the projected image has been inked-in on paper it can be used as a black and white outline or coloured in. Wax crayons or poster paints are best for blocking in large areas with colour. The church to which I belong once used this method for producing a life-size image of Goliath for a holiday Bible club. Once the picture had been produced, the children glued various items onto it to represent armour and painted them bronze, then painted the rest of the figure appropriately. It served as both a first-class visual aid and an absorbing group craft activity. It also took pride of place at a display of the children's craft at the club's family night.

Many churches, in my opinion rightly, would be most unhappy with the use of pictures of the Lord Jesus. If this is the case in your own church, it would clearly be wrong to use such images, whatever your own personal feelings on the matter. Some excellent children's books contain illustrations (even based on events in the Gospels) that avoid depicting Christ.

If you teach a teenager's group, avoid using visual aids that are designed for young children; these will probably cause them to mock, and so disrupt the Bible talk. Similarly, even some images designed for young children can undermine the seriousness of the passage that is being considered. I have seen pictures of David's battle with Goliath where David is portrayed as barely more than a toddler. In my opinion, this is not only inaccurate but is also a very trivial way (bordering on the impression of a fairy tale) to portray a serious passage that is filled with spiritual lessons.

Make sure your visual aids are visible, displayed at the right height, and positioned where people, furniture, or adults will not obscure them from view. When telling the story, remember also to make sure that you yourself do not sit in the way of the visual aids that you are using. Before the meeting, attach any pictures that you plan to use to a wall near where you intend to sit. Then, sitting in the various spaces that the children will occupy, check how easily the pictures will be seen. When doing this, remember that, apart from teenagers, most children are smaller than you are! Immediately before you begin to speak to them, you should check where the children are sitting and ask some to move if necessary so that they will be able to see properly.

'Virtual' illustrations ...
Preachers often talk about 'illustrations' in sermons. By this they usually mean incidents from real life or fiction that they quote in order to illustrate a point that they are trying to make. This type of teaching aid is very useful when telling Bible stories to children.

You may be able to quote from your own experience, or that of another believer whom you know or have read about. You might refer to a historical event, an aspect of the natural world, or an item that is currently in the news headlines. The incident that you quote could revolve around a character or event in a well-known children's book, television programme, or film. The number of subjects that you could refer to is almost limitless.

An illustration needs to be relevant if it is to be useful. There is absolutely no point in using it if it does not easily convey the point that you are trying to make. It also needs to be *concise*, and must not *take over* the Bible story. In other words, you must ensure that your talk consists mainly of the Bible story with some illustration, rather than the other way round. You only need enough detail in the illustration to make the point that you are trying to convey. An illustration for children also needs to be intelligible *to them*. This includes the need to be up to date. For example, there is no point nowadays trying to quote from the story of Robinson Crusoe to highlight some aspect of a Bible story. Few of the children will even have heard of him, and fewer still will have read the book. It would be better to quote from a modern book, or, better still, a children's television programme or film. Those who have young or teenage children themselves have a distinct advantage when it comes to teaching God's Word to children!

... and how to think of them

How can you find these illustrations? One approach is to try to think of specific illustrations for your talk as you meditate upon it. Once again, an early start to your preparation will make this easier. Illustrations may be based on an incident in your home life or workplace, a remark made to you, or something that you overhear. An item on the news, a piece of information in a television documentary, or an incident in a television drama may also trigger an idea.

Imagine that you are to explain to a group of teenagers the need to seek Christ and know him personally, and not to be content simply with knowing *about* him. I do not drive, so I could say something like this: 'I know a lot about driving. I can spot plenty of mistakes that other people make, and could explain to them what they're doing wrong. There's a car on my drive. I paid for it. But I can't *drive* it. My wife drives it instead. I've never passed my driving test. My knowledge is only theory—I don't have any practical knowledge of driving. I can't show you how to do it. I can't give you a lift. In fact, I sometimes need a lift from other people, even though I know a lot about driving, and even though I've paid for a car!'

A similar ploy could be used by describing an exciting sport that is full of thrills and spills which you know all about, but only as a spectator; or an exotic holiday location that you have heard about from a colleague or neighbour. You could find out about a particular celebrity who fascinates teenagers or children. You could mention a number of facts about the person but conclude by saying that you have no personal knowledge of him or her at all.

Thinking of the incident of Jairus' daughter, you could perhaps call to mind an incident in your life when you were very anxious to speak to somebody about a matter that was very important. You waited for the right opportunity for a few moments, but became increasingly agitated until you finally interrupted and spoke out. Some people might have considered you rude, but that did not bother you at all. The only thing that mattered was that you said what you desperately needed to say. With a little thought you will probably be able to think of various incidents in your experience or that of others that could be used to illustrate other aspects of the plight and feelings of Jairus.

Stand-up comedians often introduce a joke with the line, 'A funny thing happened on my way here tonight …' This technique should be avoided. We should be truthful, and not invent dramatic stories that we claim actually happened. Similarly, if we are quoting someone else's experience (whether that person is known to us or not), we should not claim or imply that it happened to us. Children will become sceptical if the illustrations that we use imply that we live a life that is packed with action, drama, and danger on a daily basis! They may even take the Bible less seriously as a result.

The opposite approach

It is useful to cultivate the habit of thinking through events (major or trivial) and material from books, radio, or television *as we encounter them*, to be used *at a later date*. Pausing for just a few moments to reflect on what we see and hear can be very fruitful to our own souls, and it can also supply us with material that we can use when teaching the Bible to children, especially if we make a mental or written note as these things occur. This method can, of course, be used alongside the practice of trying to think of illustrations as and when we need them.

I have always been fascinated by nature, and by animals in particular. I once read a book by a veterinary surgeon who specialized in exotic animals and whose clients included many zoos. On one occasion, he was asked to treat a killer whale that was developing sores on its dorsal fin. Both its keepers and the vet were mystified, especially because the sores seemed to appear overnight. The mystery was eventually resolved: the wounds that this large creature was sustaining came from rats! As it rested at night near the side of its pool, rats living near the poolside scampered onto its back. They chewed at its fin that stuck out above the water, causing injury and infection. I find this a useful illustration to bear in mind whenever I need to explain the folly of thinking that 'little sins' cannot cause any major harm.

In my place of work, a cheque once arrived for about £14 million. Of course, it was of no value whatever either to me or to any of my colleagues. We all looked at it, touched it, and admired it. We all thought of what we could do with that amount of money, but it was just a daydream. The cheque was payable to the organization that employed us, not to any individual among us. We were excluded from all the benefits that such a sum of money could bring. To me it was a very obvious illustration of the vastly rich blessings that are promised for all who believe—and that those who do not believe have no right to them. They can admire them from a distance only. But as long as they remain unbelieving, these blessings do not bear *their* name.

A word of caution

As with most illustrations of gospel truth, the one mentioned above has limitations. Even some teenagers would not understand how cheque payments function. Nor can the illustration be pressed too far. It can only illustrate *one or two* points. For example, it is not as if the wording on the cheque said, 'Pay to *whoever believes* the sum of fourteen million pounds.' Also, the company that sent the cheque could have instructed its bank to place a 'stop' on the cheque. They could have omitted to sign it. In either of these cases, despite the vast potential of that cheque, it would have been worthless, even to the person for whom it was intended. The more we analyse the illustration, the more complex it becomes!

Such limitations do not necessarily make an illustration useless. We only need to use it to make the specific point that we are seeking to convey. We could even consider contrasting one or two of its shortcomings with the reliability of God's promises. But both the illustration and the way in which we use it must be simple, obvious, and clear.

Some Bible truths are impossible to illustrate clearly. In fact, misunderstanding or confusion may arise from attempts to do so. Wise preachers never attempt to illustrate the doctrine of the Trinity for this reason. Doing so could not convey accurately the mystery of the existence of one God in three separate Persons. They therefore avoid either trying to think of original illustrations or using ones that other Christians have often employed.

Occasionally, we can use the imperfections of an illustration to make a point. I once showed a picture of a hermit crab to some children when trying to explain that Jesus is both God and man. A hermit crab has a soft body. To protect itself, it crawls backwards into an empty seashell so that only its head and legs are exposed, but it can withdraw almost completely if danger threatens. It is a crab living inside a shell. It will never be anything other than a crab wrapped up inside a hard casing, but at first sight it looks like a sea snail. However, when God's Son became a man, he was not a being that looked like a man but was not a man; instead, the Lord Jesus continued to be God, but he also *became* a man, with human feelings and a human personality. He went through human experiences such as joy, sadness, temptation, tiredness, thirst, pain, and even death. He was not just God's Son encased in a human body. He was, and is, both God and man. Because he is fully God we know that he is *able* to save us and help us. Because he is also fully man, we know that he understands us and is *willing* to save and help us. Using an illustration in this way needs careful handling if it is to be easily understood.

Everyday life is full of potential illustrations for children's talks or, for that matter, for sermons. We simply need to cultivate the frame of mind to recognize them, and the discipline and organization to record them for future reference. Trying to adopt this practice will prevent our illustrations from becoming predictable and boring, which can easily happen if they are almost always based on our workplace or favourite hobby.

Summary
• Make your talk visual.
• Make sure your visual aids are visible.
• Can you use any 'virtual' illustrations?

1 In the week ahead, look out in your own experience for one incident or conversation that you could use at a future date to illustrate a Bible story or biblical truth. (This could be from your home life, workplace, or place of study.) Briefly write out how you would use it in a children's talk.

2 Repeat this exercise, but this time draw the illustration from outside your own experience. (This could be from current affairs, a television drama or documentary, a novel, or magazine.)

Telling the story

My wife and children tell me that I have an annoying habit of repeating myself. There are times when I tell them things that I have already told them. Worse still, sometimes I repeat myself in the same conversation. Now that I am aware of this, I make a conscious effort to do it less, but, to be truthful, I sometimes deliberately repeat myself in order to tease them!

Sometimes, though, we *need* to repeat ourselves, to underline something that is important. Although I hope that some of the ideas and suggestions in this book are useful, they may have the opposite effect unless I mention again briefly something that I have already touched upon.

Three warnings

Firstly, we must avoid becoming proud. We may become very skilled at teaching God's Word to children, but all the skill and technique that we could ever master will produce no change in the children's hearts. We must remind ourselves continually that only the Lord can save them, and must plead with him to do this.

Secondly, we must resist discouragement, especially when we see how large a task we face, or how much is involved in sharing God's Word effectively. This book is intended to help its readers to overcome obstacles, not to make them feel inadequate. Experience and practice will improve our abilities.

Thirdly, in the previous chapter we considered how facial expressions and movements of the body can be used to add emphasis while teaching the children. We shall look at some other methods in this chapter. These should all be used sparingly. We are seeking to explain God's Word, not win an award for acting. We are seeking to attract attention to God, not to ourselves. Any methods of adding emphasis should be done too little rather than too much. If we have used some imagination during our preparation and felt the force of the passage ourselves, we may find ourselves using such methods almost subconsciously anyway. This will give a very natural feel to the way that we emphasize the various parts of the story.

With these things in mind, let us look at some more aspects of giving the talk.

Notes—or not?

Some people that I know can teach children, and even preach a sermon, without any notes at all. This enables them to look their hearers in the eye, without ever having to look down to check their place in their notes. They can also speak freely without worrying about being tied to a script.

This approach works for others, and may suit you, but it would be no good for me. I would dwell too much upon minor details in the passage, and the main points would suffer. My talk would last too long. I would forget to include something important. I would probably repeat some words or phrases often enough for it to be noticeable, possibly even irritating. I would be afraid of losing the flow of my talk as I tried to remember what I was supposed to say next. I might find myself saying 'Er … er …' or something similar, and losing the children's interest. Speaking without any notes has many advantages, but I suspect that to do so successfully requires a lot of preparation and experience, and it probably suits certain personality types best. I'd advise those who are new to teaching God's Word not to attempt it.

User-friendly notes

Other people work best with notes written out in full, continuous text. Notes like this give them a tight structure that helps them to keep to the points that they need to make, and so keeps the talk within its allotted time. I know a pastor of many years' experience who always uses complete notes when preaching, and does so for that very reason.

Complete notes also prevent important details from being accidentally missed out. Careful preparation of them enables words and expressions to be used that the children will easily understand. Full notes also enable a variety of words and phrases to be selected rather than repeating the same ones. This, too, will help to keep the children's interest. It may be the wisest choice for you for any of the above reasons, or even for a combination of them.

However, notes in complete sentences and paragraphs also present several drawbacks. Instead of looking at the children and talking directly to them, you may find yourself looking down at your notes and reading them aloud. If you do look up and make eye contact from time to time, you may find it hard, or fear that you may find it hard, to locate your place in your notes again.

One compromise is to use *abbreviated* notes. Notes like this have some of the disadvantages of each of the other methods, but some of the advantages of each, too. I write my own notes as a series of single-line, or, at most, two-line paragraphs. To help me to find my place at a glance while speaking, I indent each line from the left-hand side of the page. I have a wide range of abbreviations. Some of these are fairly standard; others would mean nothing at all to anybody else. If you are new to teaching children, try using full notes and condensed notes, and see which works best *for you*.

There is some value initially in writing out an introduction and conclusion in full; in condensed form, though, an introduction to the story of Jairus' daughter might look like this:

* what a crowd was there, to see Jesus!
* some there because the Lord Jesus famous—wanted to hear for selves!
* some because had already heard him—wanted to hear more!
* some because blind—maybe had *always* been blind!—hoping to be able see again.
* some there had not walked for *many years*.
* one man, though, *desperate* to see Jesus—more desperate than anyone else!
* hardly a moment to lose!
* had watched daughter become ill, then get worse—now dying!
* there may be time—just—but must see Jesus quickly, or all lost!
* terrible! Awful!
* pushing to front of crowd—Jairus = his name—surely nobody there in more need of seeing the Lord Jesus than he!

Some Christians are so disciplined and well organized that they complete their preparation of a Bible story several days before they are due to teach it. If you are like that, it is important to read through your notes a final time when the time to speak draws near. If you do not, your notes may have lost some of their familiarity to you, and this may prevent you speaking fluently. I like to leave writing out the final version of my notes until the evening before I am due to speak. This enables me to be entirely familiar with my material when I teach the children, and allows me to make any last-minute changes that come to mind.

Legibility, and the size of paper

Whatever form of notes you use, your writing must be neat enough and large enough for you to read easily. It is also essential that you know the meaning of any abbreviations that you have used. Lack of care here may well cause you embarrassment when you speak to the children, and break the flow of your talk.

I find it awkward to balance an unfolded sheet of A4 paper on an open Bible or, if I sit to speak, on my knee. I like to use unlined A4 paper folded in half. This gives me a folded booklet that is easy to rest on my knee or on an open Bible. Occasionally, I use several smaller sheets of paper. I once dropped such notes while speaking to the children. As they fell to the floor, they separated and scattered, and it took me a few moments to gather them up and put them back in order. Now if I use several small sheets of paper I staple them together—staples hold them more securely than paperclips.

Gaining and maintaining attention

Some children are very restless by nature; others enjoy misbehaving. When teaching them we should try to avoid reprimanding those who are not listening. The more we break off the story to say things like, 'Are you listening, John?' or 'I've asked you to sit still three times already, Katie!', the harder it will be for us to get back into telling it. The children's concentration will also be broken. You may be able to embarrass a child into sitting quietly by staring at him or her as you speak. You will need to attract the child's attention first, perhaps by pausing for a few moments in the hope that curiosity will make him or her look at you. Beyond this, it is best to rely mainly on other helpers to maintain discipline while you speak.

Some thought should be given to where both children and helpers will sit. Seating children on chairs rather than on the floor can prevent them from shuffling from one place to another, and from sitting in tight groups where they may talk or distract others. Ways should be found of minimizing any disruption during the talk, whether it is due to misbehaviour or children requiring the toilet. A system of rewarding good behaviour, especially attentiveness during the story, is very useful. Chapter 10 deals in more detail with maintaining discipline, both in the entire meeting and during the time of teaching.

If most children in the group are fairly sensible, you could try to gain their attention by asking questions as you go along, such as, 'How do you think Jairus felt when the woman who suffered a lot of bleeding delayed the Lord Jesus?' This helps to concentrate the children's minds. If some children are likely to give deliberately silly answers, invite others to answer instead.

Keeping to schedule

It is very important to have a fairly accurate idea of the time while speaking, particularly if you are likely to overrun. On the other hand, too many glances at a watch worn on the wrist can be distracting to your hearers. Placing your watch on a chair or table nearby will help you to consult it discreetly and without it being noticed by the children. As previously mentioned, thorough preparation should also help you not to overrun the allocated time.

Using the voice

It is essential that the children can hear you. When telling the Bible story you should speak slightly slower and a little louder than you would do in ordinary conversation. It is also important to pronounce words a little more carefully than you normally would. In particular, try to make sure that the end of one word and the beginning of the next word do not merge together. Ensuring that the children sit together, rather than scattered throughout the room, will help you to be heard by all. Nervousness can cause some people to speak quietly and to look down as they speak, thus muffling their voice further. Make a conscious effort to speak loudly enough, and to look up. Experience will help you to overcome nerves. So, too, will adequate preparation. If you are unsure whether you usually speak loudly and clearly enough when teaching the children, you could ask one of the other helpers after the meeting.

The voice can be used in various ways to avoid sounding monotonous. Some people have an almost musical lilt to their voices, while others speak with very little expression. Some regional accents emphasize one or other of these two effects. If you tend to put little expression into your voice, try to make a conscious effort to do so when you are speaking to the children; it is not good to share God's Word in a boring, monotonous voice. Be careful though; if you overdo it you will sound unnatural, perhaps even comical.

There may be points in the talk where you may wish to speak *a little* more quietly, or *slightly* louder, for effect. Shouting at the top of your voice is unnecessary. It may frighten young children or sound so unnatural that others will laugh. Remember, too, that if you lower your voice too much to gain effect, the children may not be able to hear what you say.

Sometimes we can alter the speed at which we speak when we are telling a Bible story. Adults usually speak more loudly and quickly when they are excited or afraid, and children do this far more noticeably. If you are explaining a passage where something amazing happened, or where some of the characters were terrified, you could speak slightly faster, and use a number of short sentences to emphasize the effect. If you are dealing with an incident where the characters concerned were puzzled, thoughtful, or confused, you could do the opposite: you could speak more slowly, quietly, and introduce some brief pauses between some of your sentences. This is also helpful when you reach a point where you want the children to take to heart some of the things that you have said.

Eye contact

If someone does not look directly at you while talking to you, you may feel that he or she is evasive and untrustworthy. Alternatively, you may conclude that the person is unconvinced by what he or she has to say, or is embarrassed by it. Although you may be willing to make allowances for shyness or nervousness on the speaker's part, you would probably feel that you would pay more attention if you felt more strongly that the speaker was addressing *you*. We do not want children to come to such conclusions while we are telling them a Bible story, so it is important to maintain eye contact with them while explaining God's Word.

You may find it hard to look the children in the eye when speaking from the Scriptures, especially if you are shy by nature. I heard of a man who, each time he preached (whether in his home church or elsewhere), looked for a friendly face in the congregation. Having found one, he would look at that person throughout his entire sermon. This must have been very uncomfortable for each unfortunate victim! There are better techniques than this if you find eye contact difficult.

You may feel slightly intimidated by the other adults who are present. Perhaps you feel, hopefully wrongly, that they are scrutinizing your performance. If so, try to look at the children instead. On the other hand, you may feel that the faces of the other adults present are friendlier than those of the children! In that case, you could look at the adults while speaking, especially if they are dotted among the children. Sometimes lack of preparation can lead to difficulty in making eye contact. The solution to this problem is obvious.

It can help to look in the *general direction* of individuals or small groups among your hearers. You could look at foreheads or just above the tops of heads, for example. You should try to make sure that you vary the direction in which you look as you tell the story, so that you do not always look at the same two or three children. Avoid jerking your head rapidly from side to side, but look instead for a few moments at a time in one direction. Experience will hopefully make it easier.

If the children are seated on the floor or on low chairs, you might find it best to sit on an ordinary chair while speaking. If the children are seated on normal chairs, it may be better to stand while addressing them. It is best to be high enough above the children to allow all of them to see you, and to be able to see all of them, without being so high that you tower above them.

Soldiering on

However experienced and skilled you may be, there will be occasions when the children's minds will be elsewhere. Some children have a very short attention span. Most become especially excited as the end of school term, or Christmas, approaches. Wet and windy weather seems to lead to high spirits in some children. Sometimes it happens that the games prior to the talk were a little too boisterous or went on too long, and there has been insufficient opportunity for adrenaline to disperse. Perhaps, as you begin to speak, you suddenly feel that your preparation has been inadequate. When you wrote them out, your notes seemed structured and well ordered. Now, to your horror, they seem disjointed. Maybe you have faced a number of personal or work-related challenges during the week and feel deflated or just plain shattered. You might even be very conscious of failures in your Christian life.

Some of these issues can be prevented, dealt with, or minimized on future occasions. But right now, as you begin to speak, they are beyond your control. Your goal and duty at this moment is simply to explain and press home the teaching of the Scriptures. What you have to say is God's own saving message. More than that, it is the method that God himself has chosen, appointed, and that he uses, century after century, to bring sinners to himself (Romans 1:16). The devil may be whispering in your ear that you are wasting your time, but you are not!

I am fully aware that this advice does not sound quite so stirring when we are actually in the situation. All we can do (perhaps after a brief, silent, possibly even desperate, prayer) is to start and to battle on, until we are through. We are not accountable for matters outside our control. But we have a duty to do our best to tell our hearers about the Lord Christ. A bad experience from time to time should not drive us to despair, either of our own abilities, or of the scale of the task. Next time we are due to speak, the children's behaviour may be better, our frame of mind more settled, and our task may prove considerably less daunting! If not, we must again seek the help of God and soldier on!

Summary
- Use notes: complete or condensed, whatever works best for you. Ensure they are easy to read.
- Read through your notes just before you are due to speak.
- Plan in advance where both children and helpers will sit for the talk.
- Make sure that the children can hear you; avoid sounding monotonous.
- Maintain eye contact during the talk, and soldier on.

1 Try to think of one specific, practical way to encourage the children at your meeting to behave better during the Bible talk.
2 Identify two areas in which you think your telling of a Bible story could be improved. For each, think of just one specific, practical step that you can take to make progress.
(This exercise could, of course, be repeated from time to time, however experienced you are.)

Any song will do?

'Worship' means different things to different Christians. Some of us use the word quite often, but would find it hard to explain what we mean by it. A dictionary might define it as the act of expressing our adoration of God and our devotion to him. This takes for granted, of course, that God deserves such adoration and devotion. The whole purpose of worship is to give honour and glory to the Lord, and to recognize his claims upon us.

Some believers almost think that the adoration of God is mainly for their sakes, not his. They measure the value of worship, particularly of songs used, mainly by the way it makes them feel, rather than by the extent to which it honours God. If we are honest, we all like certain hymns or devotional songs mainly for their tune. The tune sometimes carries us along rather than the words. If we are going to include songs of 'worship' in the format of our children's meetings, we need to consider the true nature of 'worship' and, therefore, the desirable qualities of such songs.

Praise in the Bible

What is the tone and content of passages of praise in the Bible? As I began to type this chapter, I opened my Bible roughly in the middle, but at random. Psalm 96 was before me. It begins by urging us to praise the LORD; there, at the start, is the 'covenant' name of God. Most Bibles use capital letters for the whole of this word to indicate that it is the special name 'I AM' that was first revealed to Moses. Sometimes in the English Old Testament we encounter the title 'Lord', without capital letters, which comes from a different Hebrew word with the sense of 'great one'. The name 'I AM' that was spoken to Moses and that is used most often in the Old Testament speaks of God's eternal, unchanging existence. His sovereign faithfulness to his people is also linked to this special name. Psalm 96 proceeds to talk about the LORD's salvation, glory, and great acts. It tells of his creating power, majesty, and powerful rule over all nations. It ends with the themes of his justice and his coming in judgement. It does so in clear, unambiguous language. There is nothing vague, abstract, or mystical in the way its themes are expressed.

In other words, this psalm explains *why* the LORD is to be praised. It contains elements of joy, humility, and seriousness. It connects with the mind and not just the emotions. It cranks the lukewarm or anxious heart into gear by reminding it of specific truths about God. It encourages humility and self-examination. It honours God by declaring what he is like, and its *words* help to encourage and, at the same time, challenge the worshipper. Its tone is intelligent and reverent, yet far from morbid. It could even be said that the psalm helps to *teach* the worshipper by describing what the LORD is like. It also implies that the worshipper should respond to this great God. What is true of this psalm could also be said of many other passages of praise in the Bible, whether in the New Testament or the Old.

Songs of praise for children today

If we truly want to honour God today, we will want to sing hymns and songs that follow the biblical pattern of praise. Using this as our measure, the best worship songs (whether traditional or modern) glorify the Lord by explaining what he is like and what he does. We will also benefit from worshipping him in song. The tune will have a part to play, but the profit that we gain should come primarily through the words. We should be reminded of specific truths about God that make us glad, strengthen our confidence in him, and show what he expects of us. If such elements are indeed part of the *biblical* pattern of worship, children's songs and choruses should also contain them. Obviously, children will need to sing songs that are phrased in simple language. This does not mean, however, that the songs we teach them should say almost nothing worthwhile, or say things in a silly and trivial way.

The combination of music and rhyme fixes songs in our minds. Sometimes, during our daily routine, a song that we have heard on the radio comes to mind. We may love it, we may even loathe it, but, however hard we try, we cannot get it out of our heads. At other times a hymn or chorus springs to mind. Quite out of the blue we find ourselves reminded of who God is and how much we owe him. If children learn good songs and choruses, this may happen to them, too, perhaps even long into the future.

The search for a repertoire

We should try to find songs and choruses that cover a range of topics. For example, among many songs about God the Father or about the Lord Jesus Christ, we may find one or two about the Scriptures, or about a Bible character. A good scope of biblical themes will make it easier to choose a song that fits in well with a particular passage. It is not necessary to gather a large number of songs. Although the children will soon get bored if they only ever sing the same two or three songs, they need to sing them often enough to learn them and remember them thoroughly. It is especially important that a number of short songs are sung frequently for the sake of those who cannot read well. A longer song can be taught by adding a verse each week until the children have learned it all.

Recent years have seen the production of many Scripture choruses. The content of some of these may be a little obscure for children, and some tunes can be difficult to learn, but many are very suitable. I remember a teenager whose favourite song was about the parable of the rich fool (Luke 12), with words straight from the Authorized Version of the Bible. It is thrilling to think that he may still remember this sobering passage many years later.

Many choruses and hymns say things that are only true of the child of God. This does not necessarily mean that we should not use them. After all, we sing similar types of hymns in church even though some unbelievers may be present. From time to time, however, it may be helpful to offer a word or two of explanation either before or after the song is sung. We do not want to give the impression that God saves everyone. We do not want the children to think that God automatically answers every person's prayers, nor even that he grants every single request of some people. We do not want them to think, for example, that if they pray for it, the Lord will ensure that they get the latest PlayStation for Christmas. We do not want them to assume that their prayers will guarantee the recovery of a grandparent who is slowly dying. On the other hand, we do not want to give the impression that prayer is, at best, a lottery or, at worst, a waste of time!

Can you write a song?

Your answer to this question is almost certainly, 'NO!' Your answer would probably be the same if I asked whether you, or anyone in your church, has ever considered trying to write a song. You probably wonder why you should want to!

You may sometimes wish that you knew a song about a particular character or incident from the Bible that would tie in with a syllabus of lessons. Perhaps you do not have any songs about a particular subject that is very important in the Scriptures. Maybe you simply feel that, although many of the children's songs in your collection are acceptable, few have words that are positively good.

Help for the musically challenged

If you are going to try writing a song, you may wonder whether to work on the words first and then try to devise a tune to fit, or to produce a tune first, to which words can later be penned. Either way, the idea of writing a tune seems even more impossible than producing lyrics. Like me, you may be unable even to read music.

There is an answer: an existing tune can be used. Even some well-known hymns have their origins in this method. The Irish tune 'Londonderry Air' (more commonly known as 'Danny Boy') has proved a delightful setting for at least two beautiful hymns. The hymn tune 'Boston' has the feel of a folk tune and may even have had such an origin.

Borrowed tunes can be slowed down or speeded up a little, if doing so is more in keeping with the new words. Tunes from well-known children's songs could be used for new words. 'Give me oil in my lamp' has a fairly fast and versatile tune: a new song set to its tune could consist of verses followed by the chorus (as with the original song), or *pairs* of verses, where the second verse in each pair fits the tune for the original chorus. Such tunes are easy to learn and sing. They are also straightforward to accompany. This is an important factor, especially for children's meetings held on midweek evenings when pianists may be unavailable.

The next stage

If you think of one of the tunes mentioned above, you have a starting point, a set number of lines of a specific length, along with a beat, or rhythm, to which words can be fitted. You even have a rhyming pattern that you may copy—if you choose to, for not every line needs to rhyme with another. You may also have a tune for a chorus. You have a framework to build upon. Perhaps now the idea of writing a song does not seem quite so impossible.

You may already have in mind a subject that you wish featured in a children's song. The easiest way forward is to jot down ideas for whole lines or parts of lines. Any phrases that come to mind should be scribbled down. So should any words that come to mind that rhyme together. You could get some good ideas for groups of words that rhyme with each other by browsing through a hymn book or book of children's songs. Do not cross out any of your jottings, however unpromising, in case they can be salvaged or adapted later. It can be useful to write out the original words on alternate lines, and to write your own words between them. This can help to make sure that your words fit the rhythm or beat of the tune in a natural, unforced way.

After a while, and after a few sessions of playing with your material, lines and partial verses may begin to take shape. Short sessions working on this are more productive than a single, longer period—and help to maintain freshness and prevent frustration. If you still feel that you are not making any progress, it may be worth starting again from scratch. You could try using an entirely different tune for the same theme, or stay with your original choice of tune and choose a new subject.

If a song begins to take shape, it is best to sing your words to the tune, however quietly. This will help you to assess whether your words fit the tune fairly comfortably, or whether they are forced into it. You may then need to alter some lines or rework them to fit the rhythm of the tune better. A friend may be able to help you.

A case study—the first step

Let us take 'What a friend we have in Jesus' as a model. It is an easy tune both to sing and to accompany (if we were to use a guitar we could play it in the key of D and use just three chords!).

Lines two, four, six, and eight all rhyme with one another. In fact, in the first verse, the two words 'bear' and 'prayer' are used twice, to produce two pairs of rhyming lines.

You do not need to copy this rhyming pattern, of course, but if you do, lines one, three, five, and seven of your lyrics do not need to rhyme with anything at all. Of course, you do not need to be bound by the number of verses in the original, and could choose to have just one verse, or several.

Taking the plunge

Let us suppose that you want to write a children's song about the Lord Jesus and why he came to earth. You might have got the idea from the verse '... give him the name Jesus, for he will save his people from their sins' (Matthew 1:21). A good starting point would be to try to find at least one word that rhymes with 'sins' or 'sin'. There are 'begin(s)', 'within', 'win(s)', and 'in'. You could cheat a little—many songwriters and hymn writers have done so—and use a word that almost rhymes, like 'him'.

It is easiest to begin with the lines that need to rhyme with each other, and build these lines up from words and phrases that will fit the beat of the tune. You will need to hum parts of the tune to yourself almost constantly, and fix the original words in your mind, too. This will give you a framework for how long your own individual phrases or partial lines need to be. You have not got very far yet—but you have made a start. Out of an eight-line song we have this so far:

Line 1   ... called Jesus ...
Line 2   ... from their/our sin(s)
Line 3
Line 4   ... begin(s)/within/him/win(s)

Filling in the gaps

For line two you could try 'We need saving from our sin'. That would fit the beat. Line three could be left for the time being. The ending of the fourth line needs to rhyme with 'sin'. You could try 'begin'. The idea of Jesus giving us a new beginning is biblical and helpful. He won a victory over sin and death when he died, so 'win' is another possibility. The third line and the first half of line four will probably not be long enough to move on to either of these ideas, however. What about 'within'? We all have sin inside, or 'within', us. Line three and the beginning of the fourth line may be long enough to move from the idea of 'sin' to 'within'. You could use lines three and four for the idea of our need of salvation. You could make line four something like 'for we're/they're guilty, bad *within*'. If you quietly sing these words to the tune, you will see that they fit quite well.

For line three you could try 'Everybody needs saving'. It would help the transition in idea from 'sin' to 'bad within'. It is too short for the tune. But 'Every one of us needs saving' would fit. So far this would give:

Line 1   ... called Jesus ...
Line 2   from their/our sin.
Line 3   Every one of us needs saving
Line 4   for we're guilty, bad within.

You could forget line five for now and concentrate on line six, which needs to rhyme with 'sin'. You could even 'cheat', like the original hymn from which you are working, and repeat the word 'sin' or 'within'. But having explained the need for salvation, you may wish to explain that Jesus saves us by *dying* for our sins. Line six could contain 'death/died ... victory ... win'. It will need to be tailored to the tune. You might settle for 'died, a victory to win'.

You could try some ideas for the fifth line, or move on—perhaps to the next rhyming line, line eight—and fill the remaining gaps later. This may be a good time to take a break of a few minutes, an hour or two. It may even help if you wait a few days before resuming. But as you walk to work or wait at the supermarket checkout, you could go over your words and the tune in your mind. Moments like these will help you to assess how naturally the words fit the tune. You may even get a useful idea at such times. If so, you should jot it down at the earliest opportunity so that you do not forget it. So far you have:

Line 1   ... called Jesus ...
Line 2   ... from their sin.
Line 3   Every one of us needs saving,
Line 4   for we're guilty, bad within.
Line 5
Line 6   died, a victory to win.

Line eight could end with 'him' (it nearly rhymes!), 'begin', or with one of the other words that you have already used that end in the letters 'in'.

You might like to move on to the concept of a new beginning through Jesus. Or you might want to use 'him' to end the song. The Lord Jesus does not remove everybody's guilt. He takes away the sins of those who entrust themselves to him. Line eight could be 'for all those who trust in him'. Line seven is still blank. It needs to connect the sixth and eighth lines. Line six has explained that the Lord Jesus died to win a victory. Line eight states that he won this victory on behalf of those who trust him. So line seven needs to explain what the cross was all about. Another break may be useful at this point.

Eventually, you might come up with something like this:

He's called Jesus, meaning 'Saviour',
saving people from their sin.
Every one of us needs saving,
for we're guilty, bad within.
As a man, this same Lord Jesus
died, a victory to win—
bore God's fierce and burning anger
for all those who trust in him.

This is not the most amazing Christian song that has ever been written, but it does state why the Saviour came into the world. It explains the cross, and shows the need for personal trust in God's Son. Children may possibly misunderstand the line 'bore God's fierce and burning anger', assuming it to mean that the Lord loses his temper. Depending on the age group that the song would be used for, this line may need to be reworked—or it may be possible before singing it to explain what is meant. The tune is easy to sing and to accompany, and some children may even know it already. You now need to decide whether to sing it at the same speed as the original hymn or a little faster (preferably not too fast). You also need to decide whether to try to write an additional verse or two, or whether to leave it to stand as a one-verse song. You could make a note of other suitable tunes, and a separate list of subjects or Bible characters for songs and, over a period of time, see if you can bring some together into a song.

Summary
- Check that the songs in your repertoire follow the biblical pattern of worship.
- Try to find and use songs and choruses that cover a range of topics.
- Don't be afraid to have a go at writing a song about a particular character or incident from the Bible that would tie in with your syllabus of lessons.

Putting the components together

I love to play an acoustic (non-electric) guitar, and a few years ago I was able to purchase a high-quality instrument. It far outshines those I have previously owned. I now use a very cheap guitar for Sunday school. To be honest, it is uncomfortable to play and sounds awful compared with my instrument that cost nearly ten times as much.

The top of my better guitar (where the round hole is located) is made from a single, thin piece of good quality spruce rather than from several thin layers of wood glued together. Its back and sides are similarly made from solid rather than laminated mahogany. Not only have high-quality materials been used, but all the various components have also been carefully fashioned and assembled to give the instrument a superior sound and to make it comfortable to play.

Sunday schools and children's meetings also consist of various components. Each one makes an important contribution to the club or meeting, but, as with my guitar, the way in which we use them and bring them all together can increase or reduce their effectiveness. Most Sunday schools follow a fairly traditional and semi-formal pattern. Probably the entire group gathers for a few minutes for a time of singing and prayer before dispersing into classes. The remainder of the time is devoted to teaching, possibly including the completion of a simple activity sheet or colouring picture related to the Bible passage. Midweek children's meetings or holiday Bible clubs tend to be a little more lively and rather less formal!

The prelude to the talk

Before the talk begins, the children should be encouraged to sit quietly. This is particularly important if they have been playing energetic games. Serving a drink and a biscuit may help to quieten them, but a specific period of time for this should be set and adhered to; some children can take a long time to drink a single cup of juice and to eat one biscuit. If it is your policy to run a reward scheme for good behaviour, it can be useful to remind the children as they settle down, to listen to the story. At this point children should be asked to switch off mobile phones, and any who have brought toys or games with them should be encouraged to put them away or hand them over for safe keeping until the close of the meeting.

These moments present the opportunity to underline the teaching that the children receive. We could briefly refer to the previous week's talk or story. We could remind them that the Bible is true, that it comes from God, and that we need to listen to it, believe it, and do what it says. Songs can be sung that tie in with the Bible story. Some weeks, we could comment on the content of one or more of the songs, or we could draw brief lessons from them. From time to time, an item in the news (perhaps a natural disaster, a terrorist attack, or the recruitment of a footballer for a record sum) may hit home even to children, and a few brief remarks from a Christian perspective could be made.

Prayer

Just before we pray with the children, we could briefly explain what the God to whom we will talk is like, and could mention the need to sit quietly and show him respect. We could explain *why* we are going to pray; for example, that we need to tell the Lord that we are sorry for the wrong things that we have done.

Prayer should be brief, and, as with the Bible talk, expressions should be avoided that the children will not understand. Rather than say, 'Lord, bless us through your Word', we could ask him to help us to listen carefully and to believe that what we hear is true. We could pray, 'Lord, please help us to remember what we hear. Make your Word change us and help us to say "No!" to what is wrong and "Yes!" to what is right.' Instead of simply asking God to 'forgive our sins', we could mention some specifically. When we pray, it is important to make sure that we are directing our words to the Almighty, not to the children. The temptation to aim prayers at our hearers can be particularly strong when they are misbehaving. This is such a misuse of prayer that it is not really prayer at all.

It is very easy for prayers to sound very similar every week, especially if the same person usually leads in addressing the Lord. Given the scope of teaching contained in the Bible, and given the needs of the children, it is a great pity if we repeat ourselves too much and too often. It can be useful for several helpers to take turns in offering prayer. Those who do so could give a little advance thought to what to say, and to what words and expressions to use.

Reading from the Bible

If the relevant Bible passage is usually read aloud before the story or talk, it is worth considering the best way to do this. It can be helpful for different adults, or volunteers among the children, to perform this task. If children are asked to read, those who are fairly fluent should be chosen; any who struggle with long words and who pause between each word will quickly rob the passage of its force.

There are definite advantages in asking the person responsible for the talk to read out the appropriate verses. He or she will already be familiar with the passage and will be able to read it fluently, and in a way that emphasizes the very points that will be raised when explaining it to the children. If other helpers are to read, they should ideally be asked in advance rather than on the spur of the moment. They should also be encouraged to read it through and think about it several times in preparation.

If the club or meeting is for teenagers, you may want to issue Bibles to everybody and encourage them to follow the reading. If you obtain a number of copies of the same edition of the Bible, you could announce the page number on which the reading begins. From time to time, a few moments could be spent in explaining how the Bible is made up. To do this you may need to read up about it yourself. Involvement with children's meetings can be a useful way of stimulating your own reading and understanding! You could also spend a little time occasionally teaching the children how to find their way round God's Word.

Other activities

Midweek meetings usually contain activities that are often referred to as 'non-spiritual'. For many, perhaps most, of the children who attend, this element is the main reason for coming. It has to be said that some churches encourage attendance by keeping any spiritual input to a bare minimum. Perhaps more usually, church members look on the 'non-spiritual' part of the meeting as the carrot that bribes the children to come along so that they can then encounter the gospel. It is considered a necessary evil that could be done away with in an ideal world. Some believers actually feel uncomfortable about resorting to this ploy.

We should avoid both views. Although our main goal must always be to share the gospel, there is no need for any part of a club or meeting to be unspiritual. Children easily get into mischief and even serious trouble. The provision of a club or meeting where they can enjoy themselves in a wholesome way should not embarrass us. In fact, we should be glad of the opportunity to show that fun can be had without behaving badly. A time of games also provides opportunity for the children to interact with adults who are very different from many of those with whom they have regular contact.

Choice and supervision of games

Even games can reinforce Christian standards of behaviour. You may think that I am taking matters a little too seriously, but I think it is important that any adults who take part in the games do not cheat. They should set a good example by accepting a referee's decision or by losing graciously. Those organizing or refereeing games should be fair in applying rules and making decisions.

Might equals right in the world at large, and those who succeed often do so at the expense of others. Children whose skill enables them to dominate or monopolize a game should be encouraged to be more considerate some of the time. Any adult participation needs to be kept similarly in check; the games are intended for the children, and should not be dominated by enthusiastic adults! Any reckless behaviour must be stopped, whether on the part of children or helpers.

Some games may prove unsuitable either because of their inherent nature or because of the age or personality of those who take part. A group of children in their early teens introduced a particular game at a meeting that I was leading. Teams were designated as countries. Upon an instruction from the person in charge of the game, one 'country' would 'invade' another and attempt to capture prisoners. The only permitted means of capture was dragging. The only permitted way of resisting capture was to cling to furniture or fellow team members.

After a few weeks we abandoned the game. It became too rough. There was the risk of injury to limbs, bruising, or of friction burns from the carpet. Equally importantly, modesty became compromised as clothing rode up or down when 'prisoners' were captured and dragged off. Such physical contact between adolescents of mixed gender also seemed unwise. I use this simply as an example of an activity that may be totally harmless with one age group or personality type, but that may be entirely unsuitable for another. Even our choice of games must promote wholesome enjoyment and avoid what is unwholesome.

As well as energetic games it is helpful to include quieter games that suit less boisterous children. It might even be possible to offer a choice between lively games and craft activities or board games. The club for primary school-aged children at the church which I attend does this. Crafts are very popular with some children, even some whom we would expect to prefer lively games. I suspect that few schools and still fewer homes provide much opportunity for children to make things with adult help and supervision. Some children probably value this opportunity to interact with adults and to receive praise and encouragement from them—this is sadly lacking in the home lives of many children. Crafts offer an atmosphere which children can find cosy and pleasant, and can provide helpers and children with the opportunity to chat with one another, as well as a sense of fulfilment for the children as they achieve something creative. Clubs for teenagers could consider offering board games as well as snooker, table tennis, or energetic team games.

The reality is that these so-called 'non-spiritual' activities offer opportunities and challenges for all helpers to show a godly example to the children who attend. They also provide ways to get to know the children, converse with them and show a genuine interest in them. In reality, these activities can be highly 'spiritual'.

Reinforcing the Bible story

Additional ways can be found that will underline the Bible talk. A simple and brief quiz could be held with questions based on the passage covered, and sweets awarded to the winning team. Craft activities could be devised that are based on the theme or passage for the week.

Teaching a memory text has great value. The verse needs to be chanted out quite a number of times if it is to be remembered the following week. Once again, a points or other reward scheme could encourage the children to learn it. It is better to select a brief verse that will be relatively easy for the children to learn thoroughly, than a longer one that they will only half-remember. My own preference for personal use and for use with children is an accurate, modern version of the Bible. I would have to acknowledge, though, that verses from the Authorized Version are often easier to memorize than those from a modern one. As a compromise, memory texts could be taught from the New King James Version. As mentioned previously, it has the 'feel' and structure of the Authorized Version while avoiding old-fashioned words. Here is a challenging thought: if a memory verse is thoroughly taught every week, the children will learn ten or eleven Bible verses in one term. In a year this would be trebled, even allowing for holiday breaks when the club or Sunday school may not meet. Children in a Sunday school class may even be able to learn a longer passage over a number of weeks, rather than a series of individual verses.

Safeguarding the talk

When should the Bible talk take place? The beginning of the meeting can be a helpful time, rather than after boisterous games when the children have become hot and excited. This order of events also ensures that it is awarded adequate time and is not crowded out by other activities. On the other hand, latecomers or those who need the toilet soon after arriving may miss part of it and disturb the attention of others. Some may deliberately arrive too late to hear God's Word but just in time for the start of the games.

Having the talk towards the close of the meeting can provide the chance for the children to burn off some energy first, and to sit more quietly when they have tired themselves. On the other hand, boisterous games may overstimulate the children and make them more restless when the Scriptures are taught. Some children, apparently for perfectly valid reasons, may announce that they need to leave just before the talk begins! There is the added danger that the preliminary activities will overrun and encroach on the scheduled time for the Bible story. To prevent this from happening, we must aim to start the meeting promptly. There should be a timetable for each activity, and it needs to be adhered to. If the meeting starts late, other activities will need to be cut short. Whoever leads needs to keep an eye on the clock throughout the meeting, and step in to bring an activity to a close if need be. Helpers must be gracious enough to allow 'their' slot to be curtailed, and to respect the judgement of the leader in this respect.

The hyperactivity seen in some children today may be partly due to chemicals in foods. It is interesting that many parents excuse bad behaviour on the part of their children as due to 'too many E-numbers', while making little attempt to control what they eat or drink. We need to be aware of this problem. Fizzy drinks (or squash that has not been sufficiently diluted), sweets, and chocolate that are consumed before the story may make some children very excitable. This may be a particular problem if energetic games have already made them lively. Particular care needs to be exercised if holding any kind of party for them. We cannot lament their lack of attention if we have overexcited them with vigorous or rowdy games and pumped them full of sugary foodstuffs.

It may be worth experimenting with the timing of the talk, trying out various stages of the meeting, determining which seems to work best for your own situation, and reviewing from time to time the point at which it occurs. Other solutions can often be found. The games session could begin with lively games and gradually move to quieter ones as the point approaches at which drinks are served and the Bible story is taught.

From time to time, a child may genuinely arrive after the Bible talk has started, or may have a valid reason for departing just before it begins. Nevertheless, the teaching of God's Word is our ultimate aim. It is a good idea to make it very clear that we expect those who come along to attend the whole meeting, and not simply the parts that appeal to them. Children who regularly miss the Bible talk for no obvious or valid reason should be encouraged to decide whether they will attend the whole of the meeting or none of it. If they still persist in being absent during the story but present for the rest of the activities, we may need to prevent them from attending at all for a week or two.

Summary

- Quieten the children before the Bible talk.
- Decide and review when is the best time for the talk, games, etc.
- Ensure that those who read and pray have time to prepare.
- The choice of games must promote wholesome enjoyment; as well as energetic games, include quieter games that suit less boisterous children.
- Reinforce the Bible talk in different ways, e.g. a simple and brief quiz, or teaching a memory verse.

Identify *two* problems that occur quite commonly in your children's meeting. Try to come up with one strategy to help address each problem.

Maintaining law and order

M y children used to watch videos based on characters from the book *The Wind in the Willows*. On one occasion, a snowman competition was organized for the local animal children. The rascally weasels entered the competition. When they were rebuked, because it was unfair for adults to compete against children, they protested, 'Oh, and where does it say that in the rules, then?' 'Er ... well ... there are no rules,' they were told. Their immediate response was, 'Well, if there are no rules, we can't be breaking them, can we?'

Rules

Children need to know what is expected of them, and a few brief rules should be produced and explained from time to time. They could also be displayed on a notice board, issued to the children, or included with the parental consent form that parents sign so that their children may attend. I am assuming that your club requires formal parental consent for attendance; if not, it most certainly should. Rules for teenagers could be along these lines, perhaps illustrated with an appropriate, tongue-in-cheek image, such as of a judge or police officer:

Simpler rules for younger children could consist of something like 'Three Bs—Be safe, Be kind, and Be good.' Simple computer clip-art images could illustrate the rules: a set of stairs or other potential hazard, a happy face, and a child sitting still. Rules should never be phrased in such a way that they mimic the Ten Commandments, with each beginning 'Thou shalt not ...' Such a practice dishonours God and his Word, and encourages the children to do the same.

The key word

Estate agents say that the three key elements to selling a house quickly are location, location, location! The most important tool for maintaining discipline can be summarized in a similar way: supervision, supervision, and supervision! The ratio of adult helpers to children may be dictated by legal constraints. In the UK, for example, activities held on a certain scale require registration with Social Services, and a legally prescribed number of adults must be present (see Appendix 2). Even if registration is not required, we must still act responsibly. The most obvious factor that will determine the number of adult helpers will be the number of children that are likely to attend. Other factors must also be borne in mind, however, such as the design of our premises: some buildings have many rooms and more than one storey, and each part of the building to which the children have access must be supervised.

CONSTANT AND *ADEQUATE* SUPERVISION

Enough adult helpers must be on hand from the moment the first child arrives to the time that the last one leaves. By law, 'adult' means aged eighteen or over. The absolute minimum number of helpers at any given time should be two, preferably one male and one female.

All workers should aim to arrive before the doors open to the children. It is unwise and unfair to rely entirely on others to arrive early. On a given week, one or more of these helpers may themselves be unavoidably delayed, and the level of supervision at the start of the meeting could be critically low. If a number of workers regularly struggle to arrive before the doors open, the leader may wish to consider revising the time that the meeting begins to allow them extra time. Unfortunately, some people are simply disorganized or do not see the need to be there early, and will arrive at the last minute or a few minutes late, whatever the starting time.

Some introductory games could commence as soon as children begin to appear. This helps to keep them in one place, and channels their energy at the outset; it may even encourage them to arrive on time. Individual games such as 'Simon Says' rather than team activities are best for this purpose. They allow latecomers to join in as they arrive without the need for teams to be rearranged part-way through a game.

With the obvious exception of when they are at the toilet, children should be watched at all times and in all parts of the premises. Particular supervision is needed in any potentially hazardous parts of the building. Some children run past others on stairs. Older children may like to go up or down stairs by climbing over banisters and handrails, or by jumping part-way down—such stunts are potentially dangerous, not only to those who try them but also to others who may accidentally get in their way.

If we do not keep all children occupied throughout the meeting, they may find unhelpful ways of occupying themselves. They might need to be encouraged or cajoled into joining in, or could perhaps be invited to help with clearing away. Under no circumstances must individuals or small groups of children of any age be allowed to remain in a different part of the building unsupervised. As suggested in the previous chapter, a selection of games or a choice of activities can help to ensure that different personality types are catered for.

ACTIVE SUPERVISION

Before the meeting starts, we should check for possible hazards, such as tools that have been left out. Money or other valuables, whether belonging to the church or to individuals, should be put somewhere secure. Stacks of chairs should be made safe, removed, or screened, to prevent children from climbing on them. It should be made clear that certain areas are 'out of bounds', and these should either be locked or screened off in some way.

We should always try to be one step ahead, and to anticipate what may happen. If a break for visits to the toilets usually prompts a mass stampede, we should only allow a limited number to go at any one time, and insist that others wait until their return.

Sometimes a very simple solution can be found to prevent a problem. The church to which I belong has loose chairs rather than fixed pews. Despite frequently being asked not to, some children would always walk on, or run along, rows of these chairs, and a number of seat covers were damaged. One helper made the children remove their shoes when they arrived; this allowed them to have fun without causing damage, and meant they did not need to be told off. Reducing the need for reprimanding the children also keeps workers calmer and more patient.

As the time approaches for songs, prayer, and the Bible talk, we should take note of which children are present. Some may need to be seated away from certain others and possibly next to a helper, to minimize distracting behaviour. Any children who usually visit the toilet during the story could be encouraged to go before it begins. Seating the children on chairs rather than on the floor helps to prevent them from moving around too much.

The time for the Bible story offers the opportunity for some helpers to clear away and tidy up. However, enough helpers to supervise the children and maintain discipline should be present for the talk and, ideally, should sit among the children.

Boys will be boys … and girls will be girls

Children of all ages enjoy playing rough games with one another, and never think that even rough *play* can easily lead to injuries. Teenagers resent being treated like children, but their size and physical strength are not matched by emotional maturity. They need at least as much supervision as younger children. High spirits and hormone levels can lead to accidents, serious bullying, or inappropriate behaviour towards the opposite sex. Games that are over-boisterous or that involve physical contact between members of the opposite sex are best avoided. The clothing worn by some girls may make it unwise to play certain games—we should safeguard modesty, not undermine it.

Fashion tends to draw attention to the body, especially female fashion, and teenagers will resist criticism of their style of dress. Some girls are quite naive and unaware of the likely impact of the way they dress; others deliberately dress to attract attention. It is probably impractical to impose a written dress code. It may be possible, though, for female helpers at teenage clubs to monitor the clothing worn by girls who attend, and to speak discreetly to any who dress provocatively.

If this does not work, we should look for practical steps to minimize unhelpful behaviour. For example, we may be able to encourage boys to go upstairs ahead of girls, if some girls are wearing short skirts. This needs to be done discreetly, or it will provoke the very coarseness that we are trying to avoid. All helpers should dress appropriately and modestly, whether male or female, to avoid undue attention from teenagers of the opposite sex, and to set a good example.

Consistency

All who help with the children's meeting should understand what is expected of the children, and actively maintain those standards. Your fellow workers will be frustrated if you turn a blind eye to unacceptable behaviour, or if you reprimand a child for something that does not really matter. Inconsistent standards are also unfair to the children, who need to understand what is allowed and what is not. It is especially important that all who help agree on the grounds for temporary or permanent exclusion from the club, and support any decisions made in this respect.

Discipline should only ever be enforced by adult helpers, not by older children who may help with a club or meeting. Nevertheless, some adult helpers always prefer others to reprimand children who misbehave, and may approach a co-helper or leader with words like, 'Charlotte keeps doing …' or 'John won't do such-and-such'. Although the leader or other workers may need to assist in maintaining order, all adults should play their part. If the leader is the only one who ever deals with misbehaviour, it gives the impression that he or she is the bad guy who spoils the fun that others are happy to allow. This reduces the children's respect both for the leader and for the other helpers.

Fairness

As well as being in step with one another regarding standards of behaviour, we must each try to be consistent and fair from one week to the next. This can be very difficult, especially when we are tired or when we have had a frustrating week at work. Nevertheless, we must attempt to put our personal feelings behind us and not to allow them to influence the way that we deal with the children or with one another.

Favouritism is unfair, both to the child who receives the special treatment and to those who do not. Similarly, we must not pick on certain children simply because we dislike them, or because they have angered us in the past. When we need to reprimand a child we should do it briefly (without going on and on about it), and not in a nasty way. We must never use terms of abuse. It is perfectly acceptable to say, for example, 'That was a very stupid thing to do.' It is very unhelpful to say, 'You are a really stupid boy.' Some children are called all kinds of names at home, and, while they will never thank us for reproving them, they may at least detect a difference in the *manner* in which we do it.

Tackling badly behaved children by making fun of them, humiliating them, or encouraging others to laugh at them is a form of bullying and should be avoided. It is hard to be godly when rebuking bad behaviour, but even at these times we must seek to honour the Lord Jesus.

Without intending to, it is easy to treat children of 'church' families differently from those whose parents have no connection with the church. We can find ourselves inviting the 'church' children to answer more questions than others, because they will probably know the answers. On the other hand, we may find ourselves asking them *less* often than others, in order to give those 'from outside' a chance. We can easily overlook the good behaviour of those who almost always behave well, or find ourselves telling them off for quite trivial offences that we would not even notice in others.

Getting to know the children individually will help us to distinguish between those who deliberately misbehave and those who genuinely struggle to behave well. Let us suppose that a very restless boy, named Joseph, attends your meeting. One week he amazes you, and actually sits still for about half the story. He has never sat still for as long as that before! He deserves praise and encouragement, even though others have sat far better than he has. Equally, there is no harm in telling Joseph that, having sat well this week, you hope that he will do so again next week!

Rewarding good behaviour

Some form of reward scheme helps to promote good behaviour. Points or sweets can be awarded for attendance, for good behaviour throughout the course of the meeting, and for attentiveness when listening to God's Word. We can encourage the learning of a memory verse by giving points or small prizes to those who can recite it the following week. It is important not to overlook children who are too shy to answer questions but who listen and behave well.

Points that are issued need to result in a meaningful reward. We may decide to exchange them for small prizes every week. Alternatively, when each child hands in his or her points at the close of the meeting, we could record the number in the register. At the end of each half-term or full-term session, we could then issue certificates (of several categories, to reflect the different scores achieved). Along with the certificates (or instead of them), we could give out small toys, modestly priced Christian books, or packets of sweets, the value of the award being determined by the number of points gained. It is harder to devise such a scheme for teenagers that will not offend their dignity. Perhaps a tuck shop could be organized, and points counted as vouchers towards sweets or drinks.

It is better if points are handed out as they are awarded, rather than simply written down somewhere. This helps the children to see how many they have received, and encourages them to try for more. Pieces of coloured paper or card could be used.

We may decide to award a small prize or treat to those who sit particularly well during the talk or story. If all the children have sat fairly well, there is no harm in awarding sweets to all. But if only some have sat well, it is unfair and unwise to reward all of them simply because we feel sorry that some children will miss out. Restless children will quickly realize that they do not need to try to sit quietly, and those who genuinely try to behave well will feel cheated, because their efforts have not really been recognized.

Dealing with misbehaviour

More effort should be directed into encouraging children to behave well than into finding ways of dealing with those who misbehave. Nevertheless, we need to have some means of discouraging bad behaviour, or even of punishing it.

Younger children may respond if points are taken off them, or if treats are withheld. If a party or outing is planned, it could be made clear that those who break rules seriously or persistently will not be allowed to attend. Ideally, children should be warned several times before attendance at a special activity is refused, so that they have the opportunity to improve their behaviour. Be imaginative in your warning system: for example, many children, including a number of girls, are interested in football, so a yellow warning card could be shown to those who misbehave. If they persist, they could be shown a red card, equivalent to a footballer being sent off. The red card would signify that the child is to go home and, perhaps, not attend the following week's meeting.

Dealing with intolerable behaviour

Sooner or later children may attend whose behaviour is unacceptable. Teenagers may resort to threats or verbal abuse of helpers, or attempt to intimidate them. Some children bully others verbally or physically. Others regularly cause such disruption during the Bible story that its impact is almost entirely lost. Some children offend in many or all of these areas. If such behaviour persists despite several warnings, or if a single instance is particularly serious, you need to act decisively. The leader of the club should take responsibility for this. All helpers should make sure that the leader is kept fully aware of any problems regarding discipline.

Children must not be hit, poked, prodded, pushed, pulled, or grabbed. Nor should they be held while being told off. Great care must be exercised if children are fighting and need to be separated. If possible, avoid physically separating them. If there is absolutely no alternative (for example, if physical injury is likely to result without direct intervention), use minimal restraint and let go of the child or children as quickly as possible. Even in such situations it is far preferable to hold a child by the sleeve of his or her jumper, for example, than by the arm.

It may be necessary to ban offenders from attending, at least for a week or two. Persistent misbehaviour, or even a single serious incident, may require permanent exclusion. The nature of what has occurred may justify this without the issue of any advance warning, and may also warrant informing the offender's parents. Examples of this might be physical bullying of other children, deliberate damage to the building or its contents, and threats or physical intimidation of helpers.

Decisions to exclude children are hard to make. We feel that, if anyone needs the gospel and Christian compassion and concern, it is those very children who are the most disruptive. Our sense of annoyance can make us feel guilty, and we consider that to exclude them would be a failure to show them God's love and to share the message of Christ with them.

On the other hand, our main goal is the children's salvation, not simply their enjoyment. If we regularly allow the Bible talk to be seriously disrupted, we rob all of those who attend of the chance to hear it, and undermine our primary aim. If we permit excessive and persistent bad behaviour, we also risk losing well-behaved children. There is even the possibility that some helpers will begin to dread the night of the meeting and question whether they can continue. Every factor must be considered, and each situation must be assessed on its own merits. The leader may choose to seek the views of all the workers about the best course of action, but if helpers do not all agree upon what needs to be done, a decision will be harder to reach. He or she could consult instead with one of the church officers. Whether or not they entirely agree with the leader's decision, his or her fellow helpers should support it, provided that it has been made carefully, thoughtfully, and prayerfully.

Summary

- Compile a few brief rules for the club, to be displayed on a notice board, issued to the children, or included with the parental consent form.
- All workers should aim to arrive before the doors open to the children, and no child should be left anywhere unsupervised.
- Before the meeting starts, check for possible hazards, and move money or other valuables to a secure place.
- Be consistent in discipline. Decide how to discourage/deal with poor behaviour, and encourage/reward good behaviour.
- Ensure constant supervision, and try to think of practical solutions to problems.

Working together

In most churches, whether small or comparatively large, evangelism is undertaken and sustained by the commitment of a few. I have no wish to make any feel guilty who are already heavily involved and are unable to take on more duties. Nevertheless, we should aim to be as active as we can realistically be in the service of God. For some of us, this may mean considering involvement in a new sphere of service. For others, it may mean asking whether we could commit ourselves *a little more* where we are currently helping.

Commitment

Fond memories of the past can lead to inaccurate comparisons with the present. Even allowing for this, many older believers feel that commitment in church life is at a lower level than it was in the past. Prayer meetings seem to have been much better supported a generation ago, and there appears to have been greater enthusiasm for actively serving Christ.

Undoubtedly, many believers today face great challenges and pressures, and stress within the workplace or from other directions can affect God's people as well as unbelievers. Even so, most of us have a considerably shorter working week and a more generous amount of paid holiday than our parents and grandparents experienced. Despite owning many labour-saving devices, we frequently complain that we hardly have any spare time. Some of us have perhaps begun to view our leisure time mainly as our own slot for doing our own thing. Perhaps we are in danger of seeing Christian service as an intrusion into what is rightfully ours.

You may be unable to help with a children's club or Sunday school every week, but might you be able to lend a hand once every two or three weeks? Or, though you may be unable to help for the entire meeting, perhaps you could assist for part of it. Maybe you heard that there is a need for more helpers, and turned up unannounced on one occasion. Once you were there you felt that you were not really needed, as all the tasks had been allocated to others. Perhaps you could try again, give advance notice of your intention to attend, and find out in which specific area you could be involved.

Leaders should accept all suitable offers of assistance. Volunteers who help regularly (though not necessarily every week) may make a useful contribution and might later be willing and able to assist more often. Similarly, any who would like to 'give it a try' should be welcomed and made to feel involved, but without being given so much to do that they are frightened away. Wherever possible, it is useful if each helper can be assigned a particular duty, or at least a share in one. This will encourage them to feel that they have a worthwhile contribution to make, and may strengthen their desire to continue.

Willingness

We all have different talents and personalities, and a natural liking for certain tasks. This variety of gifts is part of the Lord's provision for every local church (1 Corinthians 12:12–31), and we should try to use and develop our abilities to the full. Some of these talents may seem very ordinary and 'unspiritual', but those who are efficient organizers can be as valuable as those who can teach God's Word clearly.

If we are not careful, though, we can make excuses to avoid tasks to which we do not feel ideally suited (or, worse still, which we consider too menial for us). This calls for self-denial. There are duties in our workplaces and in our domestic lives that we dislike and that we would avoid altogether if we could, but we accept that we must perform them. It is strange that we often fail to apply the same logic in the service of God. You may feel that you are not good at supervising and assisting the children with craft activities, and feel frustrated when several children are all clamouring for help at the same time. Perhaps organizing games is not really your strong point, and you are inwardly annoyed when it is your turn to take responsibility for them.

Others may have similar feelings about the very same tasks. But if every helper only did the things that he or she enjoyed or which most suited his or her temperament, the club might soon cease to function. Just as in family life or in the workplace, service for the Lord involves occasions when all need to pitch in with whatever needs doing, regardless of our likes, dislikes, or natural abilities. Few Christians derive pleasure or fulfilment from mopping toilet cubicles or hoovering carpets, and not many volunteer for these tasks. While God's love for the cheerful giver (2 Corinthians 9:7) is expressly applied to financial giving, the Lord surely also takes delight in every ungrudging act of service.

Sometimes we simply assume that we have no ability in a particular area, when in fact we have never really tried. For years, the same person has produced take-home activity sheets for the holiday Bible club run by the church to which I belong. He was unable to do so on one occasion, and I offered to make them instead. I was nervous, as I had only ever dabbled at desktop publishing on a computer, with limited results. Much to my surprise, I was able to produce reasonably good activity sheets, and was greatly encouraged when one of the helpers asked where I had obtained them. I mention this simply to illustrate that if something needs doing in the Lord's work, we should attempt it, and put our best effort into it. We may be surprised at what we can achieve. Incidentally, if you own a computer it is worth regularly checking computer magazines for free software. I obtained some desktop publishing software by this means, registered it, and some time later was offered an upgraded version and a suite of related software at very little cost.

Delegation and volunteering

To some people, delegation is an opportunity to offload onto others unpleasant duties, or tasks that they have neglected and that now require urgent action. You may well have been on the receiving end of this in your workplace. This is not true delegation, but an abuse of position. Others go to the opposite extreme and are very reluctant to ask others to help. This reluctance may be due to a fear of overburdening them, or a lack of trust in their ability to perform the task adequately.

There is a happy medium between these extremes. Even among a small team of helpers some will have specific skills that can and should be utilized. Those who lead should be willing to delegate jobs, while still accepting responsibility for them and helping if needed. Helpers should consider volunteering to take overall responsibility for a particular task. This does not necessarily mean performing the task single-handed, and others can be invited to assist. Those who are artistic or skilled at using desktop publishing software could offer to design publicity, and those who are well organized could produce rotas. Delegation on the one hand, and undertaking delegated tasks on the other, reduces pressure by sharing workloads. It also develops skills and helps to make everyone feel that his or her contribution is worthwhile. The Bible contains a number of examples of responsibilities being delegated and shared (e.g. Exodus 18:14–27; Acts 6:1–7).

Keeping going

One of the greatest challenges of any form of Christian service is to keep going, and to keep going *for the right reasons*. It is easy to begin in a flush of enthusiasm but become discouraged or disillusioned later. It is equally possible to commence service for God from the best of motives, only to find later that our heart is not in it as it once was. There is so much to do, and so few to do it. It is hard work and we often face discouragement. Our own situations also change as time goes by, and we may feel that we can no longer help as often as we could, or cannot even help at all any longer.

Sometimes we need to view things from a different perspective, however. Nowhere does the Bible teach that serving Christ is easy or glamorous, and neither the Saviour nor the early church experienced constant success and no setbacks. When we feel disillusioned or sorry for ourselves, we should ask ourselves whether we are truly working for the Lord, or whether we are beginning to look mainly for self-fulfilment. When we feel weary, we should remind ourselves that the demands upon us are not unique but common; few churches have too many helpers. We should ask whether, if we were to give up, the club or meeting would still be able to function, or whether those who are left would find it a real struggle to continue. It may be that, after long and careful thought, we still feel that we can no longer help. In this case, we should at least try to give sufficient advance warning to allow other helpers to be found. Alternatively, we could consider gradually handing our tasks over to others and reducing our commitment as they learn and begin to fulfil the role that we have undertaken.

When we become discouraged or even disillusioned, we should be careful about confiding in others. Talking our difficulties through with a Christian friend may help us enormously, but if we regularly share our sense of frustration with fellow helpers, our despondency may spread. Leaders in particular should attempt to maintain a positive attitude. If we feel persistently or seriously discouraged it may be better to talk to a Christian friend or a church officer who is not directly involved in the running of the club.

We can all help one another to keep going by speaking a few words of appreciation for ways in which assistance has been provided, and those who teach the children will value positive feedback from other helpers. Those who lead should make a particular effort to encourage all those who help.

Reliability

Those who lead must not assume that all helpers will be present every week. Those who help will no doubt agree with this sentiment! But, whatever your role, you should take your responsibilities seriously. If you wish to help occasionally rather than every week, you should make this clear from the start to prevent misunderstanding. If you help regularly but cannot attend on a given occasion, you should notify the leader in person, and with as much prior warning as possible. Unless an emergency arises at the last minute, you should not simply fail to turn up when you are expected.

You may think that it is enough to ask someone else simply to inform the leader of your absence on the evening when the club meets, but this practice can cause serious problems to arise. On the evening in question, the leader may suddenly discover that several helpers have either not bothered to turn up or have sent messages with others that they cannot attend. There may then be an unexpected staffing shortage, perhaps only evident a few minutes before the doors open to the children. Drastic and sudden changes of plan may be needed. This extra inconvenience and frustration could have been prevented if those who did not turn up had told the leader in advance and in person.

If you are due to perform a task on a given week and find that you will be unable to do so, you should try to arrange for somebody else to take your place, perhaps offering to take his or her turn in exchange. As a courtesy, you should then notify the leader so that he or she is aware of the change in arrangements. Once again, you should take these steps as soon as possible. It is unfair to others simply to delay seeking their help to take your turn, or to ask them to do so at very short notice simply because you forgot to do so earlier. If a crisis does arise at short notice, or if you are finding it difficult to find someone to take your place, you should contact the leader and explain the situation. Leaders should be prepared to fill any such gaps themselves. They should do so willingly and without making others feel guilty. It is part of the responsibility of those who lead.

Punctuality is important. Individual circumstances vary considerably, and it can be difficult to arrive in time. You should nevertheless make every effort to do so. The best way to arrive on time is to aim to arrive slightly earlier than you really need to, to allow for any unexpected delays. Supervision of the children can be seriously compromised if a number of helpers regularly arrive late, at the last minute, or after the children enter the building. Problems can also arise if some who play a key role arrive late. The start of the meeting may be delayed. This will in turn reduce the time available for all the activities. If the Bible talk takes place towards the end of the meeting, great care will need to be exercised to make sure that it is still afforded adequate time.

The broader picture

It is sad that, in some churches, specific ministries function almost independently of the whole fellowship. Members have only a vague awareness of what is being attempted and of who is involved. The various evangelistic endeavours are all lumped together in someone's prayer at the prayer meeting from time to time, with a general request for God to 'bless them'.

It is even sadder that, in some fellowships, pastors, elders, or deacons have little knowledge of what is going on. This may be either because they do not take the trouble to acquaint themselves with the situation, or because the leaders of specific ministries do not bother to consult them or keep them informed.

LIAISING WITH CHURCH OFFICERS

The pastor or another church officer should be involved in appointing people to positions of responsibility in children's meetings. This is especially important regarding those who will teach. Similarly, if any wish to help who are not church members, the advice and approval of officers should be sought. It is vital that all those who actively serve the church have the confidence and support of the whole fellowship, and, therefore, of its appointed leaders. As we shall see in chapter 14, it is also essential that potential helpers are screened and trained in safety awareness and child protection.

Leaders of children's meetings could give copies of the syllabus and teaching rota to church officers. They should share with them any substantial concerns regarding the children who attend or those who assist. Church officers should take an active and meaningful interest in children's ministries, while at the same time allowing the leaders of those activities to do their job without unnecessary interference. It would be helpful if at least one officer of the church could meet occasionally with all who are engaged in children's ministries. This would provide opportunity for encouragement and the sharing of problems and concerns.

Pastors and other church officers should foster any gifts that are emerging in those who lead or help with children's work. Male leaders or helpers could perhaps be encouraged to lead a church prayer meeting or brief Bible study from time to time. With positive feedback and nurture, some of these may begin to develop leadership or teaching abilities that could be used more widely in the church's life. It is important to recognize that gifts often take time to develop or to reach a consistent standard. Those who do not appear at the moment to be particularly skilled at explaining God's Word may do so in the future. Church officers should look out continually for the emergence of such gifts, and encourage them patiently without pushing people too quickly or beyond their depth.

INVOLVING THE WHOLE CHURCH

The whole church should be encouraged to take an active and intelligent interest in children's ministries. I remember hearing the leader of a young people's work urging his co-workers to make sure that prayer for that work was offered at every single church prayer meeting. A copy of the teaching plan and rota displayed on the church notice board would enable interested members to pray more effectively. Perhaps from time to time a brief period within the church prayer meeting could be devoted to children's ministries. This would allow a brief overview to be given of personnel involved, activities, needs, and encouragements, as well as a time for informed, specific intercession. It might be possible to present a written or verbal review of the ups and downs of the club at the church's Annual General Meeting. All who are involved should also make opportunities to pray together on a fairly regular basis, perhaps every month. Instead of using up another evening for this, it may be possible to get together for a few minutes after a Sunday service. As well as fulfilling the obvious purpose of seeking God's enabling and converting power, praying together strengthens or helps to repair relationships between those who work together.

Some who are unable to come along in person to children's meetings may be able to produce posters and leaflets for publicity, assist with planning a syllabus, or devise lesson outlines. Others may be able to help with preparing craft activities, or lend a hand with catering for parties or occasions when parents are invited. Looking for help beyond the normal circle of workers can relieve pressure, help others to feel involved, and stimulate active interest in the children's club or meeting within the whole church.

Contact with other churches can be a useful channel for exchanging ideas and discussing difficulties. From time to time, it may be possible to arrange a joint outing, or games night. Such occasions can also be very valuable opportunities for Christian young people in small churches to meet others.

Summary

- If something needs doing in the Lord's work, we should attempt it, and put our best effort into it. Those who lead should be willing to delegate jobs; helpers should consider volunteering to take overall responsibility for a particular task.
- Don't spread despondency; rather, encourage others to keep going by showing appreciation for their help.
- Be reliable, dependable, and punctual.
- The whole church should be encouraged to take an active and intelligent interest in children's ministries.

- All who are involved in the children's work should make opportunities to pray together on a regular basis, perhaps every month.

Identify one personal strength and one weakness that is relevant to your own service for God among children. Think of one way in which your strength could be used further, and one way of improving in the area where you are weak.

The unity of the Spirit
Please read Philippians 2:1–5, Ephesians 4, and 1 Corinthians 13:1–7

You may feel that you do not need to read this chapter because all is well among the team of helpers of which you are a part. To skip this chapter would be a mistake, though, for several crucial reasons.

Firstly, many of the New Testament letters stress the importance of mutual love and harmony. Not only are Christians urged to resolve disharmony when it occurs, they are also exhorted to do all that they can to prevent it from arising in the first place (e.g. Philippians 2:5–11; Hebrews 12:15). Even though the Lord's people at Thessalonica were well known for their love, Paul encouraged them to promote it still further (1 Thessalonians 4:9–10).

Secondly, the opportunity for offence to be given and taken is never far away. Disagreements (either open, or sullenly and secretly entertained) and 'conflicts of personality' can arise almost from nowhere.

Thirdly, our inward attitudes to our brothers and sisters are as important as our outward behaviour towards them, and it is not enough simply to be on speaking terms with one another (Matthew 5:21–24).

Fourthly, even mature and hard-working believers can fall out with each other (see Philippians 4:2–3). By contrast, many of those involved in children's ministry, perhaps even in positions of responsibility, are relatively young and have not been Christians for long. The enthusiasm and energy of youth are tremendous assets in any Christian work, but wisdom and forbearance are also needed. That is not to say that young people should not be involved in active service for the Lord. Working with fellow believers to spread the gospel is an excellent way to grow in grace. But Christian growth does not happen automatically. Patience and love often grow best when they are tested and provoked!

The pressure points
Sometimes we find that our ideas are rejected, while those of other helpers are acted upon. At other times, we feel taken for granted. Others do things

that everyone else sees and appreciates; we always seem stuck with tedious, in-the-background tasks, and our contribution is not noticed. The opposite can also happen: we can resent the help of others. We consider it unnecessary, interfering, and threatening to our own role. At other times, a co-worker may speak to us rather sharply, or criticize our efforts. We are hurt, and it is hard not to return again and again in our mind to what they have said. On the other hand, fellow helpers may take to heart something that we said to them that was not intended to be hurtful or critical. Frankly, we feel that they are being silly and oversensitive.

Philippians 2 and 1 Corinthians 13 are well-known and loved by many Christians, partly because of the beauty and loftiness of the language that they contain. These passages are in fact extremely humbling and challenging to those who read them thoughtfully.

Love behaves like this ...

Love does not create, update, or repeatedly revisit a list of hurts (real or imagined) that others have committed against us (1 Corinthians 13:5). In fact, those who love are very conscious that their own sins are great and many, yet have been entirely forgiven by Christ. They view the hurts inflicted by fellow believers as microscopic by comparison. They are willing to forgive their brother or sister *for the sake of Christ* (see Ephesians 4:32). Loving people are not self-seeking (1 Corinthians 13:5); they aim to serve God, not to find personal fulfilment or win the admiration of others. This means that they neither sulk nor inwardly seethe when their ideas are not listened to, nor do they feel threatened when somebody else wants to help. Because they seek the glory of God and not the praise of their fellows, they are still able to cope when the going gets tough, and do not nurture resentment when overlooked.

The expression 'personality conflict' is a euphemism, a term that makes the reality seem less ugly than it really is. A conflict of personalities is really a clash between *people* whose tempers have begun to rise or whose patience has run out. It may flare up over some very petty difference of opinion, or it may rise from a minor annoyance. But loving people are patient and not easily angered (1 Corinthians 13:4–5). They can tolerate a lot in fellow Christians, and put up with all sorts of odd or annoying character traits in them (1 Corinthians 13:4). In fact, those whom grace has truly changed do everything they can to promote and preserve harmony with other Christians (Ephesians 4:2–3). They feel sad if they themselves have given offence, even if they did not intend to. They are willing to make the first move towards reconciliation rather than wait for others to do so (see Matthew 5:23–24 and Philippians 4:2–3, which imply that both parties have an equal responsibility to be reconciled).

Loving people are not proud either of themselves or of their achievements (1 Corinthians 13:4). They will therefore be reluctant to say or think, 'How dare *he* (of all people) say that to *me* (who am so much better)?' Such Christians will not think that they are too important to perform mundane tasks. It is strange that, although we acknowledge in prayer that we are sinners, we take offence so easily because we feel that we deserve to be treated better.

Humble people ensure that the gifts and roles of *others* are valued— after all, these talents and abilities promote the well-being of the whole church (1 Corinthians 12:4–30). Love excludes jealousy of the gifts or contributions of fellow believers. Because it is not proud (1 Corinthians 13:4), it will not act like a control freak who feels like saying to fellow workers 'Hands off! This is *my* role!'

Kindness

Those who love others go out of their way to be *kind* (1 Corinthians 13:4). This includes being supportive and appreciative (as opposed to criticizing others and taking them for granted). To show kindness is to be polite, sensitive to the needs and feelings of our brothers and sisters, and to do all that we can to avoid giving offence, even unintentionally (13:5— 'not unseemly' [AV], 'not rude' [NIV]). Because the term is so broad, it will be helpful to consider how kindness will act or react in certain situations.

We need to guard our sense of humour, especially when dealing with people whom we do not know well. Many of us accept being gently teased by a close friend, but we feel uncomfortable when a more casual acquaintance does the same. Close friends, of course, know us very well, and are sensitive to what is off-limits when joking with us, and our friendship helps to ensure that we will not take their comments personally. Even some secular employers are beginning to recognize that comments *intended* as harmless jokes can actually be hurtful rather than funny, and are devising policies to prevent and deal with such situations. If we are kind, we will be particularly wary of making fun of the appearance or behaviour of others, especially of brothers and sisters in Christ. Even gentle teasing of close friends can be overdone. I am quite short in height, and I accept the occasional joke about my size. But if I am teased about it often, or if a joke about my size goes too far, it becomes annoying and hurtful, even if it is not intended to be.

Kind people are gentle. They deal with others tenderly and patiently, even as a parent treats his or her own children (Galatians 5:22–23; 1 Thessalonians 2:7). We have already seen that we should not resent the help of others. Looking at it from the opposite standpoint, kind people will gladly offer to help, but will avoid giving the impression that they wish to muscle in and take charge.

Christians who understand kindness will avoid overburdening others if they possibly can. Leaders of young people's work who tend to leave things until the last minute themselves should not assume that others are the same, and should try to avoid asking others to undertake large tasks at short notice. As we saw in the previous chapter, we should all give as much advance warning as possible if we are unable to fulfil a particular duty. To be kind is to show consideration.

Some Christians speak kindly *to* fellow believers but are very unkind when speaking *about* them. The Lord Jesus pointed out that our words spring from our thoughts and attitudes, and are therefore an accurate guide to them (Matthew 12:34). Love focuses on the good in others, not on their imperfections. Loving people remind themselves that the imperfections in others are overshadowed by their own (Matthew 7:1–5). Love gives the benefit of the doubt and makes allowances for what is lacking in others (1 Corinthians 13:5,7). It does not enjoy harming the reputation of others by gossip or slander. By contrast, some Christians are clever at disguising the sin of malicious gossip as godly concern or as the imparting of information so that others can pray for the person concerned.

Chapter 12

How far true love can go

We need to cultivate the kind of attitude that drove the Saviour to leave heaven, become a man, and die—even death by crucifixion—as described in Philippians 2. This passage explains that our Lord had certain privileges. He was entitled to them. He is himself *God*. Yet he willingly and consciously set these rights and privileges aside when he became a *man* (v. 6). This same self-denial of personal rights for the sake of others should characterize our relationships with our fellow believers (vv. 1–5).

As if becoming a man was not a big enough step down, Christ stooped still lower. The Lord of all became a *nobody* (v. 8)! His humiliation was extreme, as he died the agonizing and scandalous death of crucifixion. Amazingly, he did all this willingly, not because he was forced into it. In this self-denial, this refusal to stand upon his rights and dignity, he is to be our role model (v. 5). His example is also intended to motivate us as we seek to follow in this hard path of denying ourselves. It was entirely fair and reasonable for the Son of God to remain in heaven and enjoy all its glories, yet he turned his back on it and chose instead this *wholly unreasonable* path of incarnation and death in the place of sinners. His path of lifelong lowliness led to glory (vv. 9–11). So, too, will ours.

If we have truly appreciated the grace of Christ, we will likewise say (repeatedly) 'No!' to privileges, rights, and to what is reasonable. We will ask ourselves, 'What can I do to help?' rather than, 'Why should *I* do this?' and we will try to perform the task cheerfully. Like our Master, we will prefer to back down rather than insist on getting our own way. We will not stand on our dignity or sulk when our ideas go unheeded or when we feel taken for granted. We must not allow the desire for recognition and praise to be our goal (v. 3). We must put the welfare, needs, and interests of fellow believers above our own (vv. 3–4).

Perhaps most strikingly of all, this love described in the New Testament is tough, determined, and persevering. To put it bluntly, it never quits (1 Corinthians 13:7). Peter mistakenly felt that he had done more than could reasonably be expected if he forgave a brother seven times (Matthew 18:21–35). We, too, often put limits on what is reasonable. But if we have appreciated the scale of God's forgiveness towards us, we must never say (either aloud or silently), 'That's it! I'm finished with her from now on!'

This love, which the unbelieving world misinterprets as weakness, is actually one of the toughest things on earth.

This duty of brotherly love is expected of every child of God, not just some of them. We have no right to plead that we cannot help the way that we feel about others. The New Testament repeatedly insists that the Christian must discipline, cultivate, and nurture godly attitudes and thought patterns. This is not easy. It requires us to train and to exercise control even over our thoughts (see Philippians 2:5; Romans 12:2; 13:14). But it is not impossible. We have all the resources we need in the Spirit of God who lives in our hearts (see Galatians 5:16–26).

How God measures us

We need to be careful as we reflect on the passages that have been outlined above. During this life we will never *fully* attain love, or, for that matter, any other Christian virtue. The same apostle who taught that genuine believers live in the light and not in darkness also emphasized that no single believer is without sin (1 John 1:5–10). When John commands us to love one another and not to love the world, we must realize that he is urging us to make this the main trend of our lives (1 John 2:9–11). He recognizes that we will never fully achieve it.

He nonetheless insists that love must be *present and clearly evident* in every child of God. It has the same characteristics (but, admittedly, to a lesser *extent*) as the love of God through Christ (1 John 3:16–20; 4:7–12). This love did not reveal itself in mere sentimentality, but in unselfish acts for the good of others, even for those who are unworthy. Ours should do the same. In other words, the Bible goes beyond simply requiring us to exhibit brotherly love. It insists that love is the measuring stick, not just of our Christian maturity, but of whether we are actually Christians at all.

The words of Paul in 1 Corinthians 13:1–3 are very sobering. It is possible to do all the *right* things for all the *wrong* reasons. Let us suppose for a moment that our abilities, virtues, understanding, achievements, and personal sacrifice outweighed those of everyone else. What would it all amount to? Mere noise, sheer worthlessness, unless it was accompanied and motivated by love (compare 1 John 4:7–8). For those who like mathematics, we could reduce Paul's words to stark equations:

Miraculous gifts – love = mere noise

Ability to declare God's Word + great and effective faith – love = 0

Alternatively, we could put it in the language of the stock exchange. Suppose we are seeking to make a good profit for the benefit of our soul. What return would we get if we invested all our energies and resources? What profit would we make if we spent our whole lifetime denying ourselves, giving away our entire wealth and at the end died a martyr's death? If these things were present but love was absent, our investment would bring no profit whatever.

Paul is not simply using exaggerated language to make a point, or describing a situation that could never actually occur. The Saviour makes a similar statement in Matthew 7:15–23. On the last day, some people will wave a list of their spiritual gifts and apparent achievements at the Judge of all the earth. Others may be impressed, but he will not be. Their attainments have arisen from proud, unconverted hearts. Their deeds will not win a favourable verdict from the Judge who weighs hearts as well as actions.

How the unbelieving world measures us

The Saviour identified this love for one another as the distinguishing mark that the *unbeliever* notices about God's children (John 13:34–35). When Christians are kind to one another, even though their social class, temperaments, ages and hobbies are very different, the world has no explanation. When believers fall out, the unbeliever concludes that they are no different from anyone else. In other words, the way in which we treat our fellow believers either underlines or undermines our message. Many unconverted people are too anxious to dismiss professing Christians as hypocrites, and ignore Christian sincerity simply because it is imperfect. This does not alter the strange but uncomfortable conclusion of God's Word, however. Both our God and the lost sinner measure our genuineness in the same way. They examine us for our love for one another.

To cultivate love in the face of challenges that test it to the limit is very demanding. Many of those whom we are to love do not deserve it. Even fellow Christians sometimes push us to the point where further love and forbearance become unreasonable. We wonder how we can possibly keep it up, and, if we are honest, there are occasions when we wonder why we should even bother. There may be times when we cannot bring ourselves to show love and patience towards a person for his or her sake. But we can still do it for the *sake and glory of Christ* (Ephesians 5:21). Kindness, compassion, and forgiveness make huge demands of us. They made even more exacting demands of the Saviour, but his grace, compassion, and continuing readiness to forgive *us* are not intended simply as an example for us to follow. They should be all the motivation that we need to love and bear with our fellow believers. 'Be kind and compassionate to one another, forgiving each other, just as in Christ God forgave you' (Ephesians 4:32).

Summary
- The duty of brotherly love is expected of every child of God, not just some of them. Follow the example of Christ.
- To cultivate love in the face of challenges that test it to the limit is demanding, but we can still do it for the *sake and glory of Christ*.

Child protection—keeping records and minimizing accidents

In view of its long history of ministering to children, the Christian church should have pioneered the protection of children. Instead, it sat back and watched secular authorities take the necessary steps. Despite the reservations that some churches initially felt, measures most certainly did need to be introduced. The provisions within the 1989 Children Act that relate to church-based and other voluntary children's activities stem largely from political concern that abuse had in fact sometimes taken place within such organizations. As if this were not bad enough, the abuse (ranging from bullying behaviour on the part of adolescent helpers through to serious and systematic sexual abuse) had remained largely undetected. Even on the rare occasions when it was reported, those who should have offered protection and help generally shook their heads in disbelief and dismissed the allegations as fanciful. When the issue of child protection policies was raised, comparatively few churches willingly adopted such policies, and most only began to comply when they had to. Sadder still is the continuing suspicion of child protection on the part of many believers. There is often a smugness and complacency, a confidence that child protection measures are really a necessary evil, because the unthinkable 'could never happen here'. Some of us have felt threatened by child protection measures, fearing that more rigorous red tape may make it difficult for us to continue to hold children's meetings.

We should see child protection as an opportunity, not an obstacle. We have the privilege of helping to protect vulnerable members of society. We also have an opportunity to demonstrate to the world at large that we take our responsibilities seriously. Many issues are involved in providing adequate protection for children. We will consider them in two chapters rather than one, and some additional information is also provided in Appendix 2.

Responsibility—and accountability

While children are in our care, we have a moral duty and a legal responsibility to keep them safe from harm. 'In our care' means from the moment they arrive until the time that they leave. It also includes any times when we escort children to or from the meeting, whether on foot or by vehicle, and occasions when we take them on an outing or for games in the park. British society is becoming increasingly obsessed with allocating blame and seeking compensation in the event of accidents or negligence. This may alarm us. We sense that, if the present trend continues, fewer voluntary organizations will be willing to organize children's activities for fear of a lawsuit. We fear that we may respond in the same way. However, if we consider a couple of scenarios, we will understand that, generally speaking, the legal situation is very reasonable, even if individuals may have unreasonable expectations.

Let us suppose that you have a ten-year-old daughter who attends a children's club. One summer evening, you drop her off and are told that the children will be taken to the park for some games. Half an hour later, you receive a telephone call to say that, although she is not badly hurt, your daughter has been knocked down by a car while crossing the road. Would you simply accept that 'these things happen', or would you ask some searching questions about how the accident had occurred? After all, the outcome could have been far worse. She could have sustained permanent injuries. She could even have been killed. You would be even more alarmed if you were not even aware that children attending the club were to be taken to the park.

Next, imagine that you are not a believer and have a seven-year-old son. You think that he is playing on the street with his friends. When you look for him you discover that he has gone with a friend to a children's club at the church a couple of streets away. You go to collect him and enter the building. All the children are listening intently to somebody teaching them things from the Bible. Although not exactly hostile to Christianity, you are a little concerned. After all, there are plenty of religious cranks in the world, and you know nothing about the church or the individuals who are running the club, and who are teaching their version of religion to your child.

Parental consent and personal records

Parental consent must be obtained for the attendance of all children (that is to say, all under the age of eighteen) who attend your clubs. If a boy comes along for the first time, brought by his friend, you should ask whether his parents know where he is and when he will be home. If there is any doubt, he should be taken home (by the friend or by two helpers) so that you can check whether his parents agree to his attendance. You should have a supply of forms to issue to parents to confirm their consent. The form should explain briefly what the club's aims are, and what its activities consist of. It would be wrong to obtain the permission of parents without briefly stating that you spend a short time each week explaining the message of the Bible. A copy of the rules of the club could accompany the form. Just as you request emergency contact details for the children, it is important that parents are given details of how to contact you should the need arise.

This is especially important if it is your custom to lock the door once the meeting begins. Parents should be informed when they receive the consent form that this is simply done to make sure that the children are kept safe while in your care. The church's landline telephone number should be given if it has one, along with at least one other contact telephone number.

Separate consent must be obtained for any outings or overnight stays as and when these take place. Full details must be given, including departure and anticipated return times. If the return is delayed, parents should be contacted as a matter of course. If cars are to be used for transporting children in connection with the club, it is important to check that the drivers' vehicle insurance covers such usage. At least two adults must be in any car transporting children, whether to or from the meeting or on an outing or overnight stay. Care and tact will be needed if any parents offer to help with transport. You do not want to offend them by implying that you do not trust them, but you must observe sound child protection practices and make certain that children are not put at risk. Leaders should check with one of the officers of the church on the terms of the church's insurance policy to make sure that the church is insured for accidents on its premises. They should also check whether additional cover should be obtained for any outings or overnight stays.

Consent forms should request such personal details of the child as date of birth, home address, and emergency contact details. Ideally two contacts should be obtained for each child, in case one is unavailable when needed. Also, request brief information about any medical conditions 'that we should know about', and quote examples such as epilepsy, asthma, diabetes, or allergies. The form should contain the assurance that any details provided will be treated as confidential and stored in a secure place. Having given such a promise, make sure you keep it. A simple record card should be completed for each child and stored securely along with the consent forms. A lockable cupboard needs to be used, and must be *kept* locked apart from when it is in actual use. At the risk of stating the obvious, keys for secure storage need to be kept safe; otherwise we make a mockery of confidentiality.

Getting forms back

Some parents forget to send these forms back with their children, or lose them. We must stress their importance, however, and issue another copy and a polite reminder. Some parents who have forgotten to provide details may come to collect their children at the end of the meeting. You could politely ask them to complete a form there and then. Alternatively, you could visit the home with a spare form and ask a parent if you could wait while he or she completes it. No child should attend for more than a few weeks without confirmation of consent and of personal details.

On a regular basis, perhaps once a year, all parents should be asked to complete another form so that you can check whether any details have changed. Some children may have changed address without your knowledge (but if you do know that a child has moved house, you should obtain the new address and check contact details right away). They may have developed a medical condition of which you should be aware, or their emergency contact details may have changed. Some parents only have a mobile phone, not a landline, and may change their telephone number frequently in search of the cheapest bill. Return of these consent forms should be treated as importantly as return of the original form issued. The forms that you re-issue should contain a request that they be completed in full, to ensure that no changes are overlooked. Any returned forms that simply have 'no change' written across them should be politely refused.

Register

A register must be kept in which each child is signed in upon arrival and signed out when he or she leaves. We must be able to account for all who are present. A register should also be kept of helpers' attendance, preferably by helpers signing themselves in and out. The person making entries in the children's register should sit near the door, so that he or she is aware of the arrival and departure of each child. Care must be taken to ensure that latecomers are registered, and that any who leave early are also signed out. Once the meeting proper begins and adequate time has been allowed for latecomers, outer doors should be locked. This will prevent any unauthorized adults from entering the building. It will also prevent children in your care from simply disappearing home without your knowledge.

If parents collect their children at the close of the meeting, the door will need to be unlocked a few minutes beforehand so that they do not have to wait outside, especially in bad weather. This situation needs thinking through. If parents wait for their children in a different room from where the activities take place, a helper should stay with them until the meeting finishes. This provides the opportunity to chat to them and get to know them. On the other hand, it reduces the number of helpers who are supervising the children.

Some children may be collected by teenage brothers or sisters instead of by parents. Teenagers under the age of eighteen who come to collect younger children are themselves children as far as the law is concerned. As such, they will themselves require supervision from their arrival and throughout their wait for the meeting to end. As we shall see in the next chapter, teenagers on our premises should always be supervised by *more than one* helper. This may have a significant impact on the number of helpers left to supervise the children in the actual meeting. One solution may be to allow parents or older siblings to wait for the children where the activities are taking place, but this may disrupt the Bible story or games that have not yet finished. Deciding which arrangements are best will require careful thought.

Other records

In addition to the register, a book should be kept in which all accidents or instances of a child being taken ill are recorded. A brief account should be entered of what happened and what action was taken to deal with it. This should be written up at the time, or as soon after the event as possible. Ideally two helpers should sign underneath the account to verify its accuracy. Any other serious incident should be recorded, such as an allegation of abuse or a serious discipline issue where a child was sent home.

Such records should be kept securely, and retained. Hopefully, they will never be needed, but they are potential legal documents. For the same reason, registers should not be disposed of once they are full, but should be retained for several years.

Accidents

Most accidents do not just happen—they are caused. Most are therefore capable of being prevented. Minimizing them is a Christian duty, and *a legal responsibility*.

As mentioned in chapter 10, a check for potential hazards should be made before the children enter the building, and necessary steps taken to make the building safe. Particular care should be taken to secure tools or other maintenance equipment such as ladders, glass, glues, paint, or other chemicals. Apart from their need for privacy at the toilet, the children must be constantly supervised, and extra vigilance is needed on staircases. Most games could, theoretically, result in injury, but any that pose a high risk should be avoided. We should also try to explain the importance of safety to the children, in the hope that they will understand why we do not permit 'play-fighting'. When the children become overexcited they become reckless. We need to be constantly vigilant!

It is important to have an evacuation procedure and to make sure that any emergency exit routes are kept free from obstructions. Should such evacuation become necessary, adults should check that no part of the building is still occupied as they themselves leave the building. Strictly speaking, the register should always be to hand throughout all activities. In the event of emergency evacuation, this would enable a roll-call to be taken to verify that all children and adults are accounted for.

First aid

A first-aid kit must be available, and one person should be given the task of keeping it stocked. Two first-aid kits would help to ensure that one is always left on the premises even if one is needed on an outing. Unless the scale of our activities requires us to register with Social Services, there is no compulsory number of trained first-aiders. It is nevertheless advisable that all who help are given some basic first-aid training. The St John Ambulance Service would be able to provide this, but should be given a donation in return. A brief first-aid session, along with training on child protection issues, could be organized occasionally. This would guarantee that new helpers are fully informed, and give existing workers the opportunity of a refresher course. Attendance at such training should be made a requirement for all new helpers.

All accidents or instances of a child being taken ill must be logged in the 'incident book'. Any minor accident or illness should be mentioned to a parent at the close of the meeting. If the child is not collected by a parent but makes his or her own way home, you should contact the parents by telephone or personal visit. In the event of a more serious accident or illness, you must contact the parents immediately. Entries in the 'incident book' do not need to be lengthy. They nevertheless need to record how the illness or accident occurred and how it was dealt with. The way in which parents were informed should also be logged, along with the time that they were contacted.

Age limits

Generally speaking, any children's club or meeting should be confined to a specific age range. Because of their circumstances, some helpers may need to bring their own children to the meeting with them, even though they are really too young. This needs to be understood by all who help, and you will either need to make some additional arrangements to accommodate these younger children, or make some allowance for their restlessness. There may be one or two other situations where you need to allow younger children to attend. As far as possible, however, the intended age range should be adhered to. This will prevent a number of problems.

If some children attend meetings for which they are too young, you will soon be presented with requests for others to be allowed to do so as well. If you accept some but not others, you will be accused of being unfair. Older children will resent the presence of any who are considerably younger, and feel that things are becoming 'babyish'. Younger children may try to take part in games but will be unable to understand the rules or what is required. This will frustrate their fellow team members. If they participate in the games, their small size may make them prone to being knocked over and hurt by bigger children when everyone is running around. It is difficult to gain children's attention for the Bible talk at the best of times, but children who are below the age limit of the meeting will be particularly restless and a source of distraction. In short, you will find that you are spending valuable resources in babysitting children who should not even be at the meeting.

Sometimes, the opposite problem arises. Older children want to attend a meeting for younger children. Again, this may be for exceptional reasons that require you to bend the rules a little. In all other cases, you should explain that you are unable to accommodate such attendance. Once you accept some, it will be hard to refuse others. Older children easily dominate games because of their size and skill, and younger children will feel left out, even though the games are actually intended for them. Those who are too old for the meeting may well prove disruptive during the Bible talk because it is aimed at younger children. Adolescents often boss younger children around. This tendency can be especially acute if they have younger brothers or sisters present. In many cases, they are used to ordering younger siblings around at home, yelling or swearing at them and pushing or hitting them, and they will probably use the same tactics on your premises. Discipline at your children's meetings is your responsibility, however, not the responsibility of teenagers who tag along.

It is common for teenage church members to help with the running of children's clubs. There is nothing wrong with this practice, provided that you always remember that the law categorizes all under-eighteens as children. In practice, the role of any helpers who are under eighteen must be clearly defined. They must not be left in sole charge of children, should not play any active role in the discipline of badly behaved children, and cannot count as official helpers if you are struggling to find enough people to staff the meeting.

Summary

- Parental consent must be obtained for the attendance of all children; update contact and medical information annually.
- All records must be treated as confidential and stored in a secure place.
- Keep a register to sign each child in and out, and to record helpers' attendance.
- Record all accidents or instances of a child being taken ill in a separate book.
- Make sure you have an evacuation procedure, and keep emergency exit routes free from obstructions.
- Keep at least one first-aid kit; one person should be given the task of keeping it stocked. Ensure that all who help are given some basic first-aid training.

Child protection— protecting from abuse

B y today's standards, the old black and white horror movies that feature Dracula, the wolf-man, or Frankenstein's monster are more amusing than frightening. When these films were made, their shock value lay more in what the villains *were* rather than in what they did. They were strange creatures, almost human but not quite. Their characters were betrayed by their appearance, which was bizarre, disfigured, or wretched.

Real-life monsters are less obvious. Who would have thought that behind the smiling face of Dr Shipman lay the mind of a serial killer? Some men who beat their wives and children wear a three-piece suit to work and are members of the local golf club. A mother may be a well-respected teacher, but destroy the self-esteem of her own children by constant nagging or by telling them repeatedly how horrible they are. Men who prey on children may be married and have children of their own. They may do the same kind of job that we do and live in a neighbourhood like ours in the next town. Most children who are abused are victimized by adults (or even adolescents) within their own family or circle of acquaintances, rather than by strangers. There are women who abuse children, but as such cases are relatively rare we will assume in this chapter that the abusers are male.

Any mention of child protection within the context of a church makes some Christians uncomfortable. They feel almost as if they themselves are under suspicion if they are expected to submit to some form of screening before being entrusted with children. In any case, they argue, surely it is unnecessary. 'No child molester could ever get through our net! They would be immediately detected when they applied for membership!' Such is their confidence.

Needless red tape?

Pædophiles often target voluntary organizations that provide activities for children. They know that such bodies tend to scrutinize candidates less thoroughly than professional organizations. Voluntary groups are often more trusting, especially if they are struggling to find helpers and suddenly encounter volunteers who appear to be both able and enthusiastic. There have been instances in recent years where paedophiles have learned evangelical jargon, convinced churches of their authenticity, and wormed their way into leading children's clubs. Those who abuse children find ways and opportunities to gain their trust as they plot to betray it in the cruellest possible way. Child protection is a necessity, not a luxury.

We glory in the power of the gospel to change the very worst of sinners. Imagine, however, the following situation. You may take delight in reading in a prison worker's prayer letter that a convicted sex offender has been converted. You give God thanks. A year later, the man is released. You do not know his identity. Without your knowing, he moves to your town, and a Christian worker introduces him to your pastor. Your pastor's thanksgiving turns to apprehension. He wonders whether the ex-convict is a genuine believer or a fake. He asks himself whether the man still poses a risk, or whether his former sins have been entirely eradicated. He wonders whether the whole church should be told, but fears the hostile and suspicious reception that the recently converted offender will meet. Your pastor is torn between trying to reconcile concern for children with a desire not to doubt the transforming power of the gospel, and compassion for a repentant sinner.

A child protection policy should include a code of conduct for dealing with situations such as this. It would ensure genuine support for a penitent offender. It might include the guarantee of confidentiality, provided that he strictly adheres to certain conditions. At the same time, it would also protect children in the church's care, including the children of members.

When we think of child abuse, we often think of sexual abuse, but there are other forms. We therefore also need guidelines for reprimanding children, and for ways to restrain them. Child protection also involves minimizing the risk of accidents, and keeping children safe from bullying or other inappropriate behaviour from other children.

A child protection policy will also protect *us*. We will hopefully avoid incidents that will cause untold grief and heartache for parents and that will implicate us. It will also protect us from false allegations. These are rare, but not unheard of. A disturbed child, or a child with a grudge, might well consider making an accusation out of spite. It might even be done as a kind of joke that quickly gets out of hand. Suddenly aware of the seriousness of what he or she has said, the child is afraid. But rather than admit to a malicious and untruthful nature, the child stands by the allegation.

In other words, far from threatening our position, child protection safeguards children, parents, and workers. To reflect the positive gains of having such a policy, the church of which I am a member refers to its policy as *childcare* rather than child protection.

Screening workers

All who help with children's work must be screened. Some churches request a signed declaration from candidates that they have no criminal convictions that would preclude their assistance. It is better to go a step further and to obtain Criminal Records Bureau (CRB) clearance. We should do this both for existing helpers and for new workers. After all, it is unfair to expect new helpers to submit to such scrutiny if existing workers have not had to do so. These checks will need to be repeated periodically to ensure that they are up to date. Candidates should not become involved in the children's work until they have been cleared.

If you have overall responsibility for a children's meeting or club, you must also ensure that all who wish to help have the approval of the officers of the church (pastor, elders, or deacons). The spiritual nature of the task makes this necessary. The leaders of your church may have different opinions from yours about the spiritual calibre of some individuals. The approval of church officers is particularly important if some wish to assist who are not members (such as students who attend your church during term time only). It is essential that, as well as posing no risk to children, these individuals are sympathetic to the doctrines taught by the church, and to the aims of your meetings. All candidates should be interviewed by an officer of the church before being appointed. The need for helpers to be in agreement with the club's aims and with the church's beliefs is an added reason for declining offers of help from older brothers or sisters of children who attend your meetings.

Titles for workers

It used to be common for children to refer to some adults in their sphere as 'Auntie' or 'Uncle'. For a child to call adults such as family friends by their first name was considered disrespectful. On the other hand, to address them as 'Mr' or 'Mrs' was far too formal. Children nowadays often call even a stepfather or stepmother by his or her first name, and almost always use the first names of their friends' parents. The use of terms such as 'Auntie' or 'Uncle' in a children's club now sounds strange to a child. To parents, it may actually sound sinister, and give the impression that we are encouraging an inappropriate bond between children and adults. This issue deserves to be thought through.

Producing a policy

Several people should produce the child protection document. At least one officer of the church should be involved, and at least one leader of children's meetings. This group of people must make all those who help with children's meetings and clubs aware of the policy and its practical implications. They must impress on all workers the need for it to be strictly adhered to. The document needs to include the issues raised in the previous chapter, such as parental consent, secure storage of confidential records, and registration of children and helpers.

Firstly, the policy must minimize risk. Particular thought should be given to any parts of our activities and practices that pose *potential* risk, whether or not anything has ever gone wrong so far. Secondly, it must be realistic. We may produce a policy that is watertight but is in fact so idealistic that we are unable to adhere to it. This brings us to the third criterion. Once we have produced the document, we must ensure that we adhere to it consistently. We make a mockery of it if we identify areas of risk, commit ourselves in writing to eliminating them, but regularly allow them to occur. We are failing in our responsibilities to the children and to one another. We are also failing in our legal duty. There is only one thing worse than having no child protection policy. It is to adopt a policy and, subsequently, to ignore it.

Leaders or helpers have no right to ignore the parts of the policy that are difficult or impossible to adhere to. If your policy is so rigorous that it is impractical, the matter must be referred to an officer of the church. It may be that the policy can be slightly amended—*provided that doing so does not compromise child protection*. It may equally be that the policy needs to be left intact and that you need to change the way in which you do things. Whichever is amended, the end result must be the same; there must be no distinction between policy and practice.

The policy needs to give particular attention to outings and overnight stays. A number of practical issues need to be addressed for such situations. Apart from minimizing accidents and preventing the potential for abuse by adults, we need to safeguard children in our care from harming themselves and one another. This could be in the form of substance abuse, bullying, or inappropriate sexual behaviour.

All those who have CRB clearance and the approval of your church must be given a copy of the policy. They should sign a document to the effect that they have understood it and will maintain it. It is useful to provide one or more training sessions on child protection (and, possibly, basic first-aid) for all who assist at children's meetings. This should be made a condition of helping in any capacity. It should *not* be considered an optional extra for helpers to attend should they wish. From time to time, it may be helpful to provide refresher courses for re-familiarization, and to enable new helpers to get to grips with the policy and the issues associated with it.

The Churches' Child Protection Advisory Service (CCPAS) has an approach that is both thorough and helpful. It produces a range of useful material and provides training seminars, support, and advice. Quite apart from their usefulness for children's meetings, the material and training courses offer some excellent tips for parents who want to teach their children how to be safe without alarming them. The address of the CCPAS can be found in Appendix 2.

Important ingredients of a policy

Whatever the ratio between male and female helpers at your club, always ensure that there is at least one male and one female present every time the club meets, and for the duration of the entire meeting. This creates an impression of responsibility and avoids causing suspicion. It is also good practice for discipline and supervision.

Somebody within the church should be appointed as a point of contact for any child protection issues. This person should not be directly involved with any of the children's meetings, in order to safeguard an independent and impartial position. If you help at any children's meeting and are concerned at breaches in the policy, or have concerns about the behaviour of any of your co-workers, you must inform the leader of the meeting. If we have any concerns about the leader we must inform the designated independent child protection supervisor. Leaders of children's meetings have the main responsibility of ensuring that your policy is adhered to. If they have concerns about any helper, they need to speak to him or her directly. Grave or continual concerns about a fellow worker should be shared with the church's child protection supervisor. In view of the spiritual nature of our task, these concerns may include matters other than child protection. It could be, for example, that a particular worker says things that are not biblically correct when he or she is teaching the children.

It is essential that we avoid any situations where one adult is alone with one child, either on the premises or off them. There should always be two adults in any car that is transporting children. The same rule must apply if children are escorted to or from the club on foot. As already stated, particular care will need to be taken on any camps or weekends away. Children's privacy must also be safeguarded while they are changing their clothes, at the toilet, or showering. As well as avoiding situations where one adult is alone with a child, always try to ensure that you have at least two helpers in charge of a *group* of children. It is better if doors made of solid wood are replaced or adapted so that the top part contains a glass window.

Some children enjoy hugging adults and sitting on an adult's knee. It is inappropriate for helpers to initiate this behaviour, which could embarrass or even alarm a child. It is best to allow a child to hug you if he or she wishes, but not to hug him or her in return. Generally speaking, children should not be encouraged to sit on an adult's knee. There will be exceptions to these general guidelines, of course. The mother or father of a young child may be present, and it is perfectly acceptable and natural for a child to sit on the knee of his or her own parent! Children who fall and hurt themselves will appreciate a hug or being allowed to sit on the knee of a helper. Wherever possible, a female helper should fulfil such roles.

Many schools do not permit parents to take photographs or video events in which children are taking part. This is done to prevent paedophiles from obtaining seemingly harmless images of children for evil purposes. However, most schools allow or make available group photographs. They usually advise parents in advance if this is to occur, so that any children whose anonymity needs to be preserved for witness protection purposes can be excluded from the photographs. It is a good idea to follow a similar practice if you wish to take and display photographs of any special children's event, for example, a holiday Bible club or a weekend away.

Great care needs to be taken in reprimanding or restraining children. A policy needs to specify methods that are unacceptable, such as smacking, grabbing, shaking, poking, or touching a child. Other forms of bullying or harassment should be identified and prohibited. Making fun of a child (even jokingly), the making of sexually suggestive comments, inappropriate touching, showing favouritism or constantly 'picking on' a child, should be specifically mentioned.

The worst-case scenario

We would all prefer not to think about the worst-case scenario. Careful thought and sound procedures are the best way to prevent it, or at least to deal with it in the best possible way. Once again, CCPAS offers some most helpful guidelines about dealing with cases of actual, suspected, or alleged abuse.

If an allegation of abuse is ever made against a worker, the matter cannot be dismissed. Neither the co-workers of the accused person nor the leader of the meeting is entitled to decide whether the allegation is true. Nor are these people qualified or entitled to look into the matter themselves. The child protection supervisor must be notified immediately. If the allegation is serious, regardless of whether the supervisor believes it or not, it must be referred to Social Services, to guarantee thorough and independent investigation. The worker in question must not be allowed to continue involvement until the matter has been resolved. When first appointed, the child protection supervisor could contact Social Services and ask for any guidance that they would like to give, for future reference.

This may seem very drastic. If your policy is sound and you adhere to it, hopefully the situation will not arise. Nevertheless, you cannot risk covering up a potentially serious offence. However awful, you must keep everything above board, and be open and co-operative in any investigation.

All who help or lead should make sure they know what to do if a child confides in them that he or she, or somebody else, is being abused. 'A friend' to whom these things are happening may even be the child's way of describing his or her own experience. Such a complex and traumatic situation cannot be thoroughly dealt with here in a few sentences. The issue must be carefully thought through and adequate procedures incorporated into the child protection policy. It is best not to tell a child outright that you believe everything that he or she is saying to you—it may be fictitious. Nevertheless, it may be true, and you must encourage the child to speak openly and frankly, and avoid appearing judgemental. You must not ask 'leading' questions that assume a certain answer. Doing so could plant ideas into the child's mind. If the allegation proved true, you could unintentionally have invalidated statements that the child had made.

If a child confides in you, you cannot promise that you will not tell anyone. After all, any alleged serious abuse must be reported and investigated. The safety of the child and, possibly, of other children, is at risk. Under no circumstances must you contact the child's parents directly about the matter. The abuser may be a family member or close friend, and could well cover his tracks if he learns that he has been discovered. The child may even be threatened into keeping silent. The same procedure must be adopted even if the alleged abuser is known to you, however shocking or incomprehensible the situation may be.

It is possible that you will encounter a child whom you suspect is a victim of abuse. Such a situation calls for enormous care and wisdom. On the one hand, we have a duty to look out for the children in our care. On the other hand, it would be all too easy for our imaginations to run away with us and for us to suspect abuse where there is none. Great trauma would be caused to families if we raised unfounded concerns about specific children. We would also bring ourselves and the gospel into disrepute. It is common practice in police forces for officers to serve on family protection units only for short periods of time before being transferred to other duties, as working in such an environment for too long can lead them to overreact and imagine abuse where there is none.

From time to time, a child may attend your meeting whose family is known to Social Services and receives support from them. If you know this to be the case, show the child—and the family—the respect and confidentiality that they deserve. Resist the temptation to tell other helpers or church members (only because you are concerned, and so they can pray, of course!). If you were that child—or, for that matter, a member of the family—you would not want to be subjected to turning heads and knowing glances wherever you went. Child protection even includes protection of privacy and confidentiality.

Summary
- Devise a child protection policy.
- Screen all existing helpers and new workers, preferably obtaining CRB clearance.
- Ensure that you adhere to the child protection policy consistently.
- Appoint somebody within your church who is not involved with the children's meetings as a point of contact for any child protection issues.
- All who help or lead should make sure they know what to do if a child confides in them that he or she, or somebody else, is being abused.

Back to basics

It seemed to me that the best way to end this book would be to return to one of the most basic truths in the Bible. We all know it. We teach it to others. But we easily forget it ourselves. It is that, although 'man looks at the outward appearance … the LORD looks at the heart' (1 Samuel 16:7). What we are inwardly is what we truly are.

As we saw at the beginning of this book, our inner desires and attitudes prompt us to commit sin. We also do things that, at least outwardly, appear to be good and noble. But the human heart is the most deceitful thing on earth, and only God can fully know it (Jeremiah 17:9–10). We must never allow busy activity for God to become a substitute for devotion to him. Working with children will soon become a mere duty or chore if we neglect fellowship with him.

If we lose touch with God we may become proud of our achievements or efforts, and we will forget that we can achieve nothing unless he changes the hearts of the children. Love for the Lord Jesus will make us long to see that power at work and pray that he will indeed bring salvation to many of them. A healthy devotional life will help to protect us from discouragement or despair, too. We will encounter characters in the Bible who kept going despite difficulties and disappointments, and we will be encouraged to ask our heavenly Father to sustain us in the same way. We will read promises that we can hold onto and that we can plead before him in prayer. Maintaining and enjoying fellowship with God will help to keep us joyful, and so combat a sense of drudgery when we feel tired or under pressure.

As outlined in previous chapters, children and teenagers sometimes stretch our patience almost to the limit. There are even times when our fellow believers exasperate us. These feelings of annoyance and frustration can easily grow out of proportion. We must nurture our tolerance and compassion by meditating on God's Word, and must ask the Lord to help us to maintain a biblical perspective when we feel angry or hurt.

Most importantly of all, the Lord *deserves* our love and devotion. It is sad that so few people in the world acknowledge this. It is sadder still when those who claim to love the Lord lose sight of it. The greatest tragedy of all is when people who tell others about God's great love are hardly moved by it themselves, because they have allowed their own hearts to grow cold over a period of time. We may one day find ourselves in such a condition. If we do, two courses of action face us.

The devil will urge us to stop being hypocrites. He will say that we should give up our involvement in children's ministry because we are not fit to continue. He will then tell us that we are such failures that we cannot possibly resume fellowship with God. He will whisper to us that if we try to, the Almighty will want nothing to do with us. We can allow ourselves to listen to him. But Satan is no friend. He is a deadly enemy who constantly plots our downfall. The more we act upon his advice, the more miserable we will feel, and the further we will drift from the Lord. The further away we slide from him, the harder it then becomes to return to him. Instead of flooding our minds with a sense of guilt, the devil may simply encourage us to become more and more careless about our relationship with God until our hearts become almost indifferent to him. The end result is the same.

Another voice speaks to us, though, if we will only listen to it. It is the voice of a Father who desires the return of his wandering son (Luke 15), regardless of how far that son has wandered or what he has done. It speaks tenderly, and promises the warmest possible welcome and the greatest joy that we could imagine if we will only return. He is eager to forgive and to restore us. In our hearts, we know that his promises are genuine and that his voice is tender.

If our hearts ever begin to wander from him, may the Lord give us grace to turn back to him and rediscover his great love! It is better to do it sooner rather than later. It is certainly better to do it now, while our hearts are still responsive, than to delay any longer.

Summary

- We must never allow busy activity for God to become a substitute for devotion to him.
- We must nurture our tolerance and compassion by meditating on God's Word, and must ask the Lord to help us to maintain a biblical perspective when we feel angry or hurt.
- If our hearts wander from the Lord, let us hear the voice of the Father

who desires the return of his wandering son, regardless of how far that son has wandered or what he has done.

Recommended resources

Teaching aids

All the publications listed below are useful for preparing to teach a specific passage. Careful study of them will also provide practical examples of the selection of simple language and of ways to introduce Bible stories, 'illustrate', and conclude them. Pastors or other mature Christians may also be able to lend or recommend commentaries or other books that deal with specific parts of the Bible. As mentioned earlier, material for younger children can often be adapted for teenagers.

THE CHILD'S STORY BIBLE BY CATHERINE VOS (EERDMANS)

This is well written and, unlike some 'story Bibles', is very faithful to the Bible passages in question. It is aimed at children of primary school age.

GOFORS AND GRUMPS BY DEREK PRIME (DAY ONE PUBLICATIONS)

A volume of biblical character studies in an A-Z format. It is designed for primary-school-age children and also includes other story-related activities.

GO TEACH/COME LEARN

A series of Sunday school and holiday Bible club material. The Sunday school material is available for separate age groups: 'primaries', 'juniors', and 'teens'. A very wide range of passages of the Bible is covered. The teacher's material suggests memory verses, gives background information, and provides a teaching aim for each lesson. Accompanying visual aids (in booklet form and on CD) and activity sheets are also available for each series of lessons. Subscription even for a year or two would result in a considerable stock of teaching material and visual aids for later use. You can find out more about them at http://www.goteach.org.uk or by contacting: The Christian Bookshop, Sevenoaks Road, Pratt's Bottom, Orpington, Kent, BR6 7SQ.

LESSONS FOR LIFE BY JILL MASTERS (WAKEMAN)

Four books of teaching material that cover most of the narrative parts of the Bible as well as some biblical themes. These can be used or adapted for young children through to teenagers.

LEADING LITTLE ONES TO GOD BY MARIAN SCHOOLLAND (BANNER OF TRUTH)
An excellent young children's book based on a topical approach rather than a series of connected Bible passages, although most chapters are based on a specific passage. Memory verses are suggested for each story.

THE LIFE OF JESUS BY C. MACKENZIE (CHRISTIAN FOCUS PUBLICATIONS)
A topical book aimed at primary school-aged children about the life and ministry of the Lord Jesus based around questions such as 'Why did Jesus come into the world?' and 'Why did Jesus have to die?' This book appears to be currently unavailable, but it might be possible to buy second-hand or to borrow a copy.

PARABLES OF JESUS; PEOPLE JESUS MET BY B. RAMSBOTTOM (GOSPEL STANDARD)
These books are aimed at primary school-aged children. They contain no pictures of Jesus, are beautifully illustrated, and are faithful to the Bible record of events. Other titles deal with the birth of the Lord Jesus and his resurrection. These books are very reasonably priced and, besides being useful source books, make good-value prizes.

YOU MIGHT HAVE ASKED ... BY STUART OLYOTT (EVANGELICAL PRESS)
This asks and answers the kinds of questions that many teenagers ask.

DAY ONE PUBLICATIONS
DayOne producse some excellent Bible-story colouring books that would make helpful visual aids or prizes. Their Bible-text pens and pencils also make cheap but attractive prizes, as does their range of bookmarks containing Bible verses or a list of the books of the Bible.

Understanding the Bible

Any Christian who is serious about understanding the Bible should have a copy of William Hendriksen's *Survey of the Bible*, published by

Evangelical Press. It states the theme of every Bible book, and provides an outline of each one, as well as giving a wealth of background information.

InterVarsity Press have published several editions of Bible dictionaries. Besides being useful teaching aids, these can be of enormous personal benefit. A good starting point would be to look up some of the key words in the first chapter of this book, such as righteousness, sin, redemption, and justification.

In the first chapter we briefly considered part of Paul's letter to the Romans. This book of the Bible gives some of the clearest teaching in all Scripture about the gospel and about living the Christian life. Stuart Olyott's book *The gospel as it really is*, published by Evangelical Press, is extremely helpful. It is one of the Welwyn commentaries, a series of brief but thorough commentaries on various books of the Bible.

Grace Publications have produced an excellent series of condensed and modernized 'Christian classics'. Some of these explain important truths found in God's Word, others describe aspects of Christian living. Because they have been very heavily condensed to a fraction of the size of the original books, they need to be read a little at a time, and thoughtfully. Hopefully, some of these simplified versions will whet your appetite to read the full editions. A helpful way of getting to grips with one of the original versions is to read it a chapter at a time, using the simplified one as a guide to it.

Clip art and visual aids

As well as the material available from *Go Teach* mentioned above, the following UK websites are also worth visiting. As well as supplying graphics to illustrate Bible stories, they also provide useful clip art for publicity purposes.

http://www.wesleyowen.com

http://www.cc-art.com

Typing a criterion such as 'Christian clip art' into your Internet search engine should also provide you with a number of useful sites

Child protection issues

Relevant UK legislation

In chapter 14, we considered the need for an effective child protection policy. In the UK, this is actually a requirement of the 1989 Children Act. To highlight the implications of this, it may be helpful to consider a specific scenario. Suppose (however awful it is to do so) that a member of a church like yours, or somebody connected to it, is found guilty of abusing a child while on its premises and during the club. The members of that church could be held corporately liable for damages and court costs awarded to the child and to his or her parents. The logic is simple: it is the responsibility of that church to ensure that children in its care are kept safe. Whether we think in terms of safety from serious accidents or safety from abuse, the law's expectations of us are the same.

It is only right that the law now requires a far more responsible approach towards children while they are in the care of churches and other voluntary organizations, especially when we reflect that the naivety and laxity of such groups has failed children in the past. It is equally fair that the law holds voluntary organizations accountable for the welfare of children in their care.

The Children Act deals with almost every conceivable aspect of child care and welfare, not just church or other voluntary children's activities. Explanatory guidelines were published in 1989 by HMSO ('Introduction to the Children Act 1989') and by the Home Office in 1993 ('Safe from harm'). The latter document presents procedures or guidelines that should be incorporated into any child protection policy. Some bookshops act as agents for HMSO/ government departmental publications; otherwise they are available through many bookshops or directly from: TSO, PO Box 29, Norwich, NR3 1GN, www.opsi.gov.uk

In Chapter 14, we considered the need for a person within the church to be appointed as, effectively, a child protection co-ordinator. This person should make sure that he or she is fully aware of the current legal requirements, *and also aware of changes in these requirements as and when they occur.* Upon payment of a subscription, CCPAS offers, in addition to other services (see below), regular updates on relevant changes in legislation. If you do not subscribe to this service, you must take other steps on a regular basis to ensure that you find out about any such changes. As mentioned in Chapter 14, it would be a good idea for the child protection supervisor to make contact with Social Services upon appointment, and to ask them for any useful information and guidelines for future reference.

Legislation changes frequently, and I am reluctant to state current requirements in case they have changed by the time you read this. It is important, however, that you are aware of the following points:

• Activities that exceed a specified total duration (number of hours per session and number of days per year) require registration with Social Services. At the time of writing, the point at which this registration is required is for an activity that lasts for more than two hours and more than five days per year. For example, a holiday Bible club that runs for six days and for two hours per day, or for five days for three hours per day must register with Social Services.

• This registration includes a number of issues:

(a) inspection of premises

(b) Social Services undertaking of the necessary CRB (criminal records) checks

(c) mandatory staffing levels, including a specified ratio of the number of helpers per child, a specified ratio of helpers over the age of 21, and the possession by at least one helper of childcare experience recognized by Social Services.

• In view of the degree of involvement required by Social Services, registration will need to be undertaken well in advance of the activity being planned, not left until the last minute!

The Churches' Child Protection Advisory Service

As mentioned in chapter 14, the Churches' Child Protection Advisory Service (CCPAS) produces a number of excellent publications, including training packs. It also offers training seminars and an advisory service. Its approach is thorough and sane, and its work is supported by the Association of Chief Police Officers.

You can contact CCPAS at: http://www.ccpas.co.uk, CCPAS, PO Box 133, Swanley, Kent, BR8 7UQ

One particularly valuable item produced by the CCPAS is a folded card containing useful telephone numbers (as well as space for recording others), along with some brief guidelines on child protection. These cards can be issued to all workers and, as they are the same size when folded as a credit card, they can be kept in a purse or wallet. It should be stressed—as CCPAS itself emphasizes—that these cards are *not* intended to serve as a substitute for a child protection policy.

If your church does not yet have a formal child protection policy, other churches in your area might be able to give you a copy of theirs that you could adapt. Using such documents as a basis would save considerable work drafting one from scratch, and would help to ensure that no important issues are overlooked. The CCPAS website (see above) provides guidance and a basic checklist for preparing a policy, as well as other useful information.

Day One Publications have published a book, *Insight into anguish*, that is a moving and, at times, harrowing account of a Christian family caught up in the trauma of serious but unfounded sexual allegations against the father. Part of its value lies in the way in which it demonstrates the need to minimize the risk of false allegations against those involved in Christian children's meetings.

Sam in the Crimea

A VICTORIAN ADVENTURE BASED
ON THE CRIMEAN WAR

NORMAN COOK

PAPERBACK, 96PP, ILLUSTRATED

ISBN 978–1–84625–045–3

Join Sam Clarke and Carrots the donkey as they hide on board a ship bound for the Crimea … Follow them through the streets of Constantinople, where Sam and his new gypsy friends take on cut-throats and bandits. Lie low in the 'Valley of Death' as they witness the Charge of the Light Brigade and encounter Florence Nightingale. This sequel to Sam and the Glass Palace keeps you reading right to the end!

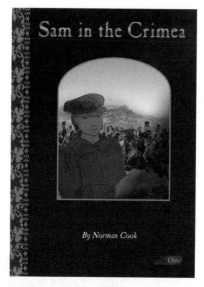

Sam and the glass palace

A VICTORIAN ADVENTURE BASED ON THE WORK OF
LORD SHAFTESBURY

NORMAN COOK

96PP PAPERBACK, ILLUSTRATED

ISBN 1–903087–42–0

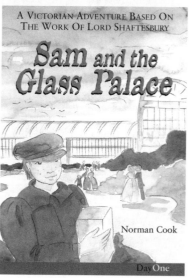

Sam Clarke was an orphan, forced to run the streets of London, desperately needing an education and, above all, new parents to take care of him. After coming into contact with Lord Shaftesbury, his dream started to come true. But then it started to become a nightmare …

32 PAGES A4 WORKBOOK

This series of colouring books will enable children to explore the Bible and learn Bible texts. The youngest child will have fun colouring the illustrations in each book—while an adult can help them to take their first steps in biblical knowledge.

CB01: THE OLD TESTAMENT
ISBN 978–1–903087–16–9

CB02 THE NEW TESTAMENT
ISBN 978–1–903087–17–6

CB03 GENESIS ISBN 978–1–903087–18–3

CB04 ABRAHAM ISBN 978–1–903087–19–0

CB05 MOSES ISBN 978–1–903087–20–6

CB06 JACOB ISBN 978–1–903087–21–3

CB07 JOSEPH ISBN 978–1–903087–22–0

CB08 RUTH ISBN 978–1–903087–23–7

CB09 DAVID ISBN 978–1–903087–24–4

CB10 NEHEMIAH ISBN 978–1–903087–25–1

CB11 MARY ISBN 978–1–903087–43–5

CB12 JOHN THE BAPTIST
ISBN 978–1–903087–44–2

CB13 THE STORY OF PETER
ISBN 978–1–903087–45–9

CB14 THE STORY OF PAUL
ISBN 978–1–903087–46–6

CB15 THE PARABLES ISBN 978–1–903087–47–3

CB16 MIRACLES OF JESUS
ISBN 978–1–903087–48–0

CB17 PEOPLE IN THE LIFE OF JESUS
ISBN 978–1–903087–49–7

CB18 PEOPLE IN THE LIFE OF PAUL
ISBN 978–1–903087–50–3

CB19 THE APOSTLES ISBN 978–1–903087–51–0

CB20 HEBREWS—MEN OF FAITH
ISBN 978–1–903087–52–7

Bible discover and colour

ANIMALS, PLANTS, BIRDS AND PLACES
OF THE BIBLE (FOUR WORKBOOKS)

PHILIP SNOW

The pictures in these colouring books are great fun for children to colour in, and each page contains a Bible quotation as well as some interesting information on the places, flora or fauna illustrated.

ISBN 1–903087–88–0 ANIMALS
ISBN 1–903087–89–9 BIRDS
ISBN 1–903087–90–2 PLACES
ISBN 1–903087–91–0 PLANTS

Reading your Bible
A starter's guide

GAVIN CHILDRESS
AND AUDREY DOOLEY

112PP, PAPERBACK, ILLUSTRATED

ISBN 1–903087–41–4

The Bible is the best known book in the world. Sadly, although most people have one at home, it often remains on the shelf unread. This short book outlines key details and facts of each book of the Bible. Illustrated throughout with fun pictures and diagrams.

A BOOK OF READINGS BASED
ON THE LIFE OF ABRAHAM

A BOOK OF READINGS BASED
ON THE LIFE OF JAMES

TIM SHENTON

TIM SHENTON

76PP BOOK, LARGE A4 FORMAT

76PP BOOK, LARGE A4 FORMAT

ISBN 1–903087–72–4

ISBN 1–903087–61–9

Does God answer prayer? What are the promises of God? How can we deal with temptation? These are some of the subjects answered in this study guide for the young. Full of interesting stories and examples that younger readers can relate to in their own lives, each chapter in this book ends with points for thought and prayer, making it a superb tool for enriching the spiritual lives of young people.

Here is an excellent devotional for young people and families. It draws out many lessons to be learned for everyday life, and points to Jesus Christ as the Saviour of the world and the friend of sinners. Includes points for thought, prayer, and memory verse suggestions.

Living4God

WILLIAM TYNDALE, JOHN NEWTON,
ERIC LIDDELL, DAVID BRAINERD

KATH DREDGE

72PP BOOK, ILLUSTRATED

ISBN 1–903087–28–7

A concise book containing biographies of four
'heroes of the faith' to inspire young Christians
today: William Tyndale; John Newton; David
Brainerd; Olympic athlete Eric Liddell.

**'Contains great lessons for us all and is
thoroughly recommended.'**
GRACE MAGAZINE

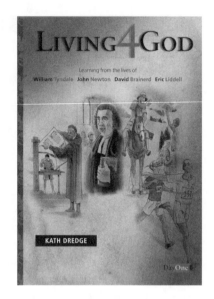

In the footsteps of the past

John Bunyan

ANDREW EDWARDS AND
FLEUR THORNTON

32PP LARGE-FORMAT
BOOK, ILLUSTRATED

ISBN 1–903087–81–3

How a hooligan and soldier became a preacher, prisoner and famous writer

William Carey

ANDREW EDWARDS AND
FLEUR THORNTON

32PP LARGE-FORMAT
BOOK, ILLUSTRATED

ISBN 1–846250–12–9

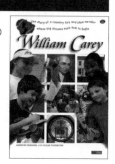

The shoemaker whose passion for Jesus brought the Bible and new life to millions in India

William Booth

ANDREW EDWARDS AND
FLEUR THORNTON

32PP LARGE-FORMAT
BOOK, ILLUSTRATED

ISBN 1–903087–83–X

The troublesome teenager who changed the lives of people no-one else would touch

William Wilberforce

ANDREW EDWARDS AND
FLEUR THORNTON

32PP LARGE-FORMAT
BOOK, ILLUSTRATED

ISBN 1–84625–028–5

People like Wilberforce relied totally on God for strength and courage … and look what he managed to achieve!

Gofors and gumps

DEREK PRIME

176PP HARDBACK, ILLUSTRATED

ISBN 1–903087–97–X

All the letters in the alphabet are used to describe Bible characters. Superbly illustrated in black and white, this is an ideal gift for teaching the young.

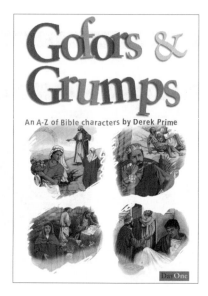

TIM SHENTON

LARGE FORMAT (A4) ILLUSTRATED BOOK, 76PP

ISBN 978–1–84625–014–9

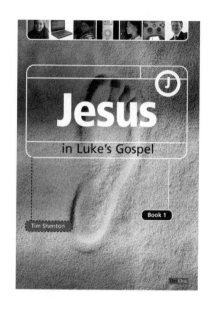

There is no greater life to study than the life of Jesus—and if we rolled all the world-famous celebrities into one, then the person who came out would be nothing in comparison with Jesus! Tim Shenton works through Luke 1–6, drawing out the main points and applying them relevantly to our modern, fast-paced life. Includes things to think about, questions to consider, action points, and a memory verse for each section.

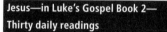

Jesus—in Luke's Gospel Book 2—
Thirty daily readings

TIM SHENTON

LARGE FORMAT (A4) ILLUSTRATED BOOK, 76PP

ISBN 978–1–84625–048–4

Who is Jesus? What did he do? Why did he come? Is it worth following him? As he answers these questions and many more, Tim Shenton shows us that there is no one like Jesus. In another thirty readings, he works through chapters 6 to 11 of the Gospel of Luke, drawing out the main points and applying them relevantly to our modern, fast-

paced life. He also suggests things to think about, questions to consider, action points, and has a memory verse for each section.

Tim Shenton is the head teacher of St Martin's School and an elder at Lansdowne Baptist Church, Bournemouth, England. He is married with two daughters. He is author of several other books, and two other booklets for younger readers—*Readings from James* and *The life of Abraham*, both published by Day One.